SCOTT AND GOETHE

Sir Walter Scott, from Sketch made in Court
by Robert Scott Moncrieff.

SCOTT AND GOETHE

GERMAN INFLUENCE ON THE WRITINGS OF SIR WALTER SCOTT

BY

REV. W. MACINTOSH, M.A., PH.D.,
RECTOR OF ST PAUL'S CHURCH, KINROSS

WITH A FOREWORD BY

J. M. BULLOCH, M.A., LL.D.

KENNIKAT PRESS
Port Washington, N. Y./London

SCOTT AND GOETHE

First published in 1925
Reissued in 1970 by Kennikat Press
Library of Congress Catalog Card No: 71-113340
ISBN 0-8046-1026-6

Manufactured by Taylor Publishing Company   Dallas, Texas

CONTENTS.

Introduction ... ... i.

German Influence on the Writings of Sir Walter Scott 1

Scott's First Acquaintance with German. His Translation of German Ballads and Dramas 5

Goetz Von Berlichingen 19

German Influence on Scott's Early Poetry, especially in "The Lay of the Last Minstrel" and "Marmion" ... 26

Germans and Germany 39

Scott's German Secretary, Heinrich Webber. Scott's Interest in German Romances and Translations from these 44

James Skene of Rubislaw 51

German Influence on Scott's Novels ... 58

"The Antiquary" (1816) 63

"The Legend of Montrose" (1819) ... 83

"Ivanhoe" (1819) 93

" The Monastery " (1820) 101

" Kenilworth " (1821) 107

" Peveril of the Peak " (1823) 113

" Quentin Durward " (1823) 116

" St Ronan's Well " (1823) 126

" The Betrothed " (1825) 128

" The Talisman " (1825) 130

" Anne of Geierstein " (1829) 135

" My Aunt Margaret's Mirror " (1827) ... 137

Scott's Novels in Germany: Goethe's
    Opinion of them 152

Scott's Correspondence with Goethe ... 173

Conclusion 192

Appendix I. 200

Appendix II. 206

Appendix III. 212

FOREWORD.

In acceding to my very old friend, Dr Macintosh's desire for a preface to his book, I wish it to be understood that I come as a learner, and not as an expert on the subject which he has made his own by many years of intensive study. It is perfectly true that ever since I read John Hill Burton's romantic *Scot Abroad*, sent into the world in its delightful roxburghe binding just sixty years ago, I have been intensely interested in those daring migrations which our countrymen made to every country in Europe and, later on, to every corner of the world, the ardent genealogical pursuit of some particular family having led me into many bypaths untraversed by Burton. The reflex action of foreign countries, especially that of France, on ourselves has been fascinating when expounded by a Michel, but this interaction has been far less studied. In particular the effect of the old Germany, after having been given an exaggerated importance by Carlyle, has suffered of recent years, owing to many causes, from underestimate.

In the process, for which a thoroughly materialised Germany has had itself largely to blame, it has needed a good deal of courage to re-adjust the balance, but in taking his courage in both hands, and putting his intimate knowledge of German to use in revaluating it, Dr Macintosh confers a debt on readers who are anxious to get at the truth of things.

In the first place, Dr Macintosh represents that type of Wandering Scholar who, with his Album Amicorum, knew no frontiers in his search for knowledge. It must be nearly half a century since I first remember him coming to my extraordinarily alert father's house, a bright, spectacled young man, intensely keen on betterment under somewhat discouraging circumstances. After he left Aberdeen, long, long ago, he first went to England and to the Continent, and then settled in Kelso, where his friendship with Robertson Nicoll was to open the road for myself to London. We saw little or nothing of each other, but every now and then I heard of his venturings, and they were always on the track of those old Wandering Scholars, ever eager and receptive and formative: and now in his autumn, on the romantic shores of Loch Leven, almost half-way between his native Bon Accord and the Border which brought him out, he remains as eager as ever, but with more time on his hands to co-ordinate his stores of knowledge, accumulated by much reading and by an intimate acquaintance with life in Germany.

It will be noticed that Dr Macintosh makes no attempt to re-assert the Carlyle position, which looked to the older Germany and to Goethe in particular, for a social and philosophical code to be followed unswervingly. The Goethe who mattered to Scott was the first of those three Goethes who followed each other. It was the Goethe of romanticism, not Goethe the classicist, nor Goethe the philosopher, and even then it affected only Scott's literary outlook, and never his personal code, which, so far as foreign influence was concerned, had far more affinities with France. The mysticism inherent in the Goethe of all moods said nothing to the realist Scott, nor could he possibly have read Novalis, who had such a profound influence on George MacDonald, whose sense of romance finds itself, in this the year of his centenary, almost entirely represented for the younger generation by that sense of faerie which Scott did not attempt to realise.

It isn't that Dr Macintosh claims to have made a new discovery. Seeley, to mention only one, pointed it out long ago. What the present book does is to fill in the interstices of the wide generalisation, ultimately showing how the wizard of Waverley passed Goethe's earlier way of looking at the past through the alembic of his own mind. This is done by a careful examination of twelve of the novels, and we are also shown how his highly idiosyncratic revaluation of the Goethe method reacted on contemporary Germans themselves. That was a task well worth undertaking, and Dr Macintosh has made it very interesting to everybody.

J. M. BULLOCH.

45 Doughty Street, London, W.C. 1.

NOTE.

I am grateful to Dr Bulloch for his kindly Foreword, and for recalling the days of Auld Lang Syne. His father, the late John Bulloch, Founder and Editor of *Scottish Notes and Queries*, Author of *George Jamesone, the Scottish Vandyck*, etc., was the friend of my youth who first led me into the fairyland of books, and from whose wisdom and knowledge I profited much in the pursuit of literature. Thus both to father and son I am under literary obligations.

I wish to express my thanks also to the Editor of the *Kinross-shire Advertiser* for kind permission to reproduce the articles which chiefly make up this little book.

W. M.

INTRODUCTION

German Influence on English Literature from Sebastian Brant to Goethe : from Alexander Barclay to Sir Walter Scott.

English literature has enormously affected the literature of Germany. The genius of Shakespeare has impressed itself on the minds of German people to almost as great a degree as on the minds of English readers. Every German readily acknowledges this, but the influence of Germany on our literature has also been considerable. Here I wish to point out in a very cursory manner how some of the greatest authors have been inspired and influenced by German literature, especially about the period in which Scott lived.

Towards the end of the 15th century there was published in Basel a work by a native of Strassburg that quickly attained international fame. The work was called " Das Narrenschiff," or " Ship of Fools," and the writer was Sebastian Brant. He introduces 113 different kinds of fools who are conducted on a great ship to " Narrogonien." Brant uses " Narrheit " in its widest, scriptural sense, almost equivalent to godlessness. He lashes the vices of all classes, but especially those of the rich. He praises poverty as the mother of all virtues, and contentment as the source of all happiness. Brant died in 1521 in his native city, where a monument is erected to his memory. His poem, which is written in the Silesian dialect, has gone through many editions, a critical edition having appeared as late as 1891.

Copies of the book wandered to this country ; the popular satire of the poem suited the temper of the times, and it was soon put into an English form. In 1509, the first year of the reign of Henry VIII., an English translation was published from the hand of Alexander Barclay, a native of Scotland, who became a priest and monk of Ely, and subsequently a Franciscan at Canterbury. His version is entitled '' The Shyp of Folys of the Worlde.'' It is an imitation rather than a translation of the original, and is perhaps of no great literary value, but it suited the period and had a remarkable popularity. Its biting satire on the vices and follies of the rich and powerful was as much needed, perhaps more needed, in this country as in Germany. For long the book retained its popularity, and there are several references to it by the dramatists belonging to the end of the 16th and the beginning of the 17th century. It has a certain value for historians, for the pictures that it gives of familiar manners and popular customs. Its chief worth for us at present is that it is the first direct example of German influence on English literature, and therefore deserves to be mentioned here. The latest edition of Barclay's work was published in 1874, when a

critical edition appeared in London in two volumes with
a life of the author, so that it is still considered worthy of
study by English scholars.

In the course of the 16th century, Germany made her
influence strongly felt through the new ideas of the Reformation. The works that came from Germany then
were chiefly theological, and not of great literary value,
except the hymns and spiritual songs which were translated and imitated by English writers. English people
who are interested in the history of religion recognise that
the Church owes a debt of gratitude to the German
reformers in this respect. The Reformation in England
and Scotland produced no sacred singers, but Germany
seems to have burst into melody at this time, and the
reformers encouraged each other with songs in their
battle for spiritual freedom. They were led by Luther
and his friend Ulrich von Hutten, Justas Jonas, Paul
Eber, Hans Sachs, and others. In a remarkable poem
Hans Sachs hailed Luther as the "Nightingale of Witten-
berg."

If anyone looks over the " Gesangbücher " used in the
Churches of Germany, he will be struck by the fact that
the great majority of the hymns had their rise in the 16th
century, or early part of the 17th century, and were undoubtedly inspired by the Reformation. The story of
Christian hymnology in Germany is most interesting, but
here I merely point out that the English Church has since
the Reformation persistently translated and formally
adopted all the best hymns which Germany has produced.

In the "English Church Hymnal" I have counted 22 German hymns which are sung in our churches to-day. In Duffield's "English Hymns" (American), there are 56 from German sources; in Schaff's "Christ in Song," we have as many as 92; in the "Church Hymnary" of the Presbyterian Churches in Scotland there are 35. We have not only borrowed the hymns, but in many cases the tunes along with them. This is a kind of influence that is more than literary; it is spiritual, and touches the heart and affects the life.

Not till the time of the Wesleys can we be said to have had any English hymn writers, and John Wesley drew much of his inspiration from Germany. He translated as many as 40 German hymns for his followers, and his collection of 1737 was the first published collection for the use of the Church. Apart from this religious-literary influence, for several decades it cannot be said that there was any direct influence made on English literature by Germany.

Then there was the "Eulenspiegel," with its somewhat unpleasant adventures by the combative Pfarrer von Kalenberg, and the "Grobianus," that had already appeared in the "Ship of Fools," and wherein the customs of 1605 were represented by Dedikind and Scheid through an English translation. The character of Grobianus appears in the extravagant Oxford comedy in which we have an account of the betrothal of the daughter, the beautiful Grobiana. This importation was little calculated to give Englishmen a favourable impression of German life and manners. Indeed, all references to Germany at this period show that Englishmen looked upon Germans, not as a nation of thinkers, but as a nation of drinkers, and that the great tun at Heidelberg was one of the chief sights of Germany!

What Shakespeare thought of the Germans of his day may be seen in the character of the German suitor for the hand of Portia in the " Merchant of Venice." It is not a flattering description, but it must be said that the adventurers from the other countries are not spared, and that the peculiarities of the Englishman are hit off with equal sarcasm and severity.

But there was another view of the German character that prevailed in England during the Shakespeare period. Germany was not only the land of measureless beer ; it was the land of witchery and mystery. In the latter half of the 16th century there arose before English eyes the gloomy form of the great magician, the immortal Doctor Faust, which Christopher Marlowe, following the story found in an old Volksbuch, made the subject of a tragedy. He has given us the life and death of the unhappy wizard, and made Faust and his arch-tempter Mephistopheles as familiar to the England of Queen Elizabeth as they were in Germany. The Faust tragedy is the most important contribution made from the great storehouse of German legend to English literature. It presented Germany in quite a different aspect ; as a kind of fairy-land, full of nymphs and gnomes, its woods peopled with Männchen and Erdgeister, and the land full of knights and squires, and fair women and brave men, whose doings were erratic and mysterious.

This was as far from the fact as the other extremes represented in a tragedy by Henry Glapthorne, who, in his " Albertus Wallenstein," published in 1639, a few days after the death of Wallenstein, has given a caricature rather than a picture of the great soldier whom Schiller was to immortalise. Wallenstein appears in this English author as a theatrical, blood-thirsty personage, who causes the death of one of his own sons and the son's lover.

This period witnessed the first of our many royal alliances with Germany. James VI. gave his daughter Elizabeth in marriage to a German Prince, which marriage led to the introduction of the Hanoverion dynasty into England.

In the 17th century Englishmen could find no literary impluse in a country desolated by the thirty years war. It was a barren time also in England, for under the first Stewart kings the French influence was paramount. The plays of Shakespeare were exchanged for translations and imitations from the French drama. There was a considerable lowering of taste and laxity of manners, which had a disastrous effect on our literature. Such men as Dryden yielded, although against his better judgment, to the prevailing taste. It was a rebound from the extreme severity of puritan times, and this liberty, which deteriorated into license, was inimical to the advancement of true literature. The French influence was carried far on into the 18th century. Even after the revival of German literature in this country, English people could hardly be induced to give an ear to German authors. Germany was torn inwardly by many political forces, and as a political power it had become weak, so that England from her insular seclusion and security, looked down on her Teutonic cousins, and despised the language and the literature. Englishmen could not be blamed when they had before them the example of Frederick the Great who treated with contempt the language of his own subjects.

Still, in spite of these facts, there were in the second half, and especially in the last decades of the 18th century, a considerable number of translations of German poems and prose works. These were, however, for the most part translated, not from the German text, but from French versions. In dramatic literature the plays of Kotzebue, which were familiar to Sir Walter Scott, had a remarkable vogue. One of his pieces, '' Die Spanier in Peru,'' was in 1799 put on the English stage by the famous actor Sheridan, and other dramas became popular. His '' Menschenhass und Reue '' long asserted its place on the English stage. So numerous were the dramas imported from Germany at this time that anxious critics spoke of a threatened German invasion, and bewailed the profanation of the stage of Shakespeare by foreign pieces in which moral lessons were sacrificed to sentiment and feeling. Even the youthful Byron in his first satire (1809) thought it necessary to warn his countrymen against the "Mummenschanz" of the German drama. We shall see how Byron himself afterwards came under the German spell.

Bürger's ballads became well-known, especially his "Leonore," as shown by the number of translations that appeared from time to time. Scott was fascinated by their weird beauty and did his best to make their merits known. It was Scott's friend, Henry Mackenzie, the author of "The Man of Feeling," who perceived the coming greatness of German literature. On the 21st of April, 1788, he delivered a lecture to the Royal Society of Edinburgh on German literature, which roused the greatest interest in literary circles. "Germany," he said, "in her literary aspect, presents herself to observation in a singular point of view, that of a country arrived at maturity, along with the neighbouring nations, in the arts and sciences, in the pleasure and refinements of manners, and yet only in its infancy with regard to writings of taste and imagination. This last path, however, from these very circumstances, she pursues with an enthusiasm which novelty inspires, and which the servility incident to a more cultivated and critical state of literature does not restrain."

It is no exaggeration to say that this lecture was epoch-making in its results. The lecturer praises the dramatic skill of Schiller as evidenced in the "Robbers," and expresses his belief that with a better subject to work upon he was destined to be a great dramatist. Yet all Mackenzie's knowledge of the "Robbers," and the other dramas of which he speaks, had been gained through French translations. Nevertheless, the lecture was the means of setting many to acquire a language the mastery of which promised such a great reward. The interest excited in Scotland spread to England, which always lags behind the northern half of the island in initiative thought ; what Scotland thinks to-day, England thinks to-morrow!

The literary historian will pursue with interest the reception each of the single authors found in England, and will trace their effects on individual writers. We can here only point out facts that lie on the surface as suggestions for more minute study. Amid the crowd selected as representative of the reception accorded to others, we mention the names of Goethe and Schiller. These great men made no triumphal entry into England. They had to fight their way against English prejudices, and Goethe in a higher degree and for a longer period than his friend Schiller. The recognition of the genius of these men was retarded by the incapacity of the translators. The prose works suffered less in this regard. Goethe's " Werter," which first found its way into England through the French, had an extraordinary popularity, although its moral tone was condemned by English censors. It was dramatised, parodied, imitated ; and we learn that even pictures from scenes in the story adorned the walls of English homes, the picture of Lottie cutting bread for her little sisters being a prime favourite. Thus in the description of a sitting room of a well-to-do English farmer George Crabbe says :—

> Fair prints along the papered wall are spread;
> There, Werter sees the sportive children fed
> And Charlotte, here bewails her lover dead.

This popularity had the disadvantage in that Goethe was long known to English readers only as the author of " Werter," while his later and riper works were overlooked. Similiarly, Schiller's juvenile drama of the " Robbers," which was early translated, was prejudicial to the poet's fame in England. The powerful conservative section in England looked upon the " Robbers" as dangerous to the state, and strove with all its power against its popularity by caricatures of the German drama. In this mockery and contempt, Goethe's " Stella " shared the same fate as the " Robbers."

The German poets received more justice with the rise of the new poetic school in England. The artificial and pseudo-classical school of Dryden and Pope began to be superseded by the romantic school, and by those simpler and wiser spirits that led men back to nature. It was the romantic school that may be said to have in a measure naturalised German poetry. The leaders in this movement were Byron and Shelley and Sir Walter Scott, who occupies a unique position, belonging, as he does partly to the old and partly to the new era. The representatives of this school recognised in the German poets kindred elements. In the last year of the century, Scott, who had practised his hand on the ballads of Bürger and others, took a higher flight when he published a translation of Goethe's " Götz," and this had an extraordinary influence on the trend of his own genius.

Lord Byron, whose " Manfred" shows the influence of " Faust," confessed his indebtedness to Goethe, and expressed his admiration for him as the man who created the literature of his own nation, and lent splendour to the literature of all Europe. When a mere boy Schiller's " Robbers" came in his way and fired his imagination. He made use of the story of the Sicilians in Schiller's " Geisterseher" for a ballad. It is believed, also, that the well-known Byronic hero, the gloomy misanthropist, who is capable of a great and passionate love and of every crime, was modelled after the pattern of one of the Epigoni and the robber Karl Moor.

The poet Shelley, was, as might be expected, attracted to " Faust," some of the scenes of which he translated into English. He not only gives us a poetical translation of the Prologue, but a literal prose translation, and then remarks : " Such is a literal translation of this remarkable chorus ; it is impossible to represent in another language the melody of the versification ; even the volatile strength and delicacy of the ideas escape in the crucible of translation, and the reader is surprised to find a *caput mortuum.*"

The interest excited in German literature was not confined to the works of Goethe and Schiller. Klopstock, Wieland, Lessing, Voss, were all well known, and it is amusing to read some of the judgments passed by critics in this country on the various writers and to compare them with the opinions held to-day. For example, one writes: " I should certainly say that ' Wallenstein ' and ' Mary Stuart ' are superior to ' Götz ' or ' Tasso ' as dramas. I might also be inclined to allow that Voss's ' Louise ' is equal, if not superior to ' Hermann and Dorothea ' ; that Schlegel's critical acumen is superior either to that which is indicated by the strictures on Hamlet in ' Wilhelm Meister,' or by the general criticism which Goethe poured forth in early life, in the journal published at Weimar, to which Schiller, Wieland, and Herder contributed ; or which in later years, he inserted in the *Berliner Jahrbuch*. Perhaps, too, I might be inclined to admit that as an elegiac writer Goethe is inferior to Matthison or Salis ; and as a ballad writer to Bürger. But looking to the vast extent of his literary labours, and viewing him as a universal genius, I am convinced that he has been scarcely ever equalled, and seldom rivalled by any writer in any land."

The writer of this criticism was Dr. John Strang, of Glasgow, who made an enthusiastic study of German literature, and published "Tales of Humour and Romance from the German of Hoffmann, Langbein, etc." He made a pilgrimage to Germany, visiting all the great writers of the time, to whom he seems to have had introductions. He had a letter of introduction to Goethe, but unfortunately Goethe was indisposed at the time and he failed to see the great man. He visited the grave of Rabener, whom he calls the German Swift, probably in reference to

Rabener's "Geheime Nachricht von D. Jonathan Swift's Letzen Willen." Strang also visited Ludwig Tieck, who said he was the first to introduce Sir Walter Scott to the German people, and he gives an amusing description of the evening parties at Tieck's house. ("Germany in 1831.")

Klopstock was another name that was well-known and highly revered by a certain class. His "Messiah" was especially popular among religious people, who hailed him as the German Milton. His poetry was considered a powerful counteractive to the supposed evil tendencies of Goethe's writings.

It is difficult to give an adequate idea of the interest that was excited in England, and the expectations that were raised regarding the new literature springing up in Germany that promised so much. Some treated this literature with scorn; others were enthusiastic, but all intelligent persons were interested in it, and Germany became a country worth visiting. Reviews of German books began to appear in the principal magazines. The "New Monthly Magazine," which was edited by the poet, Thomas Campbell, opened its pages to translations from contemporary authors, and gave reports of new publications appearing in Germany. Campbell himself was especially interested in German literature, and had spent the winter of 1800-1 at Altona, near Hamburg, where he met the hero of his "Exile of Erin."

Two other English poets made a pilgrimage to Germany to learn something more of the people and the new literature. These were Wordsworth and Coleridge, who visited the country in 1798. The promised land did not yield them all they anticipated. In Hamburg they called on the aged Klopstock, whose views on the state of German literature were not encouraging. Klopstock praised Wieland, who in his opinion, could not be surpassed by any author, not even by Goethe. As for Schiller, he was but an imitator of the extravagant Shakespeare, and was still more extravagant; Schiller would soon be forgotten, added Klopstock. In spite of this judgment Coleridge and Wordsworth were both drawn to Schiller; the former addressed a sonnet to him, and presented to the English people a poetic translation of "Wallenstein." It is said that Coleridge also planned a translation of "Faust," but on "moral grounds" gave up the task. He was of opinion that the English people would not read such an extraordinary work. The first English translation of "Faust" was published in 1823, and was the work of Lord Leveson Gower, who also translated Schiller's "Song of the Bell"; since then the number of English versions of "Faust" is legion. It may be noted that two early translations were by Scotsmen and both published in Edinburgh in 1834, two years after Goethe's death. The one was by Professor J. S. Blackie, and the other by D. Syme.

Wordsworth spent a winter in Goslar in the Harz, but seems unlike his friend to have been little influenced by German life and literature. He wrote poetry while he was in Goslar, but the subjects were English, and the scenes were taken from the Lake country. Coleridge received a lasting impression from his visit. He read deeply in German philosophy, especially Schlegel, whose philosophy coloured all his subsequent thought. Coleridge was looked up to as an authoritative guide in German literature and philosophy. He had studied at Cambridge, and it was at Cambridge that he found his most ardent disciples, among whom were Arthur Hallam, Alfred Tennyson, and other clever young men at the University.

While English poets recognised the value of German writings, and especially its chief poets, the professional critics and the most influential journals and magazines were beginning to show hostility. Goethe especially was very unfairly treated, and on many occasions his genius decried. We may cite here only one instance. Thomas de Quincey, a most prolific writer in many departments of knowledge, a master of English prose, and a man of great but eccentric genius, professed to have studied the literature and philosophy of Germany, and was therefore competent to pass a judgment on the same. The value of that judgment may be gathered from the fact that he declared that the " Sorrows of Werter" was Goethe's best work, and that Goethe's fame would sink until it had reached its proper level ; Schiller on the other hand, was praised by De Quincey as the greatest of German authors, who also as a man was entitled to more respect than any other author of modern Germany.

It was time for some one to arise who could interpret

truly the value of German literature and show its real significance. That man appeared, and he was a Scotsman—Thomas Carlyle. A Scotsman, perhaps, can best understand and appreciate German genius in its finer aspects. The Lowland Scotsman, as Carlyle was, is racially more akin to the German than the inhabitant of England. The inhabitants of England are a mixed race, having been subject to many foreign influences, of which the Norman invasion was the greatest; while the northern half of the island has been comparatively free from foreign influence. "Only a Scotsman can understand us Germans," said Goethe himself, and he acknowledged that he had found his best interpreter and German literature its greatest champion in Thomas Carlyle.

Carlyle did right yeoman service, and never wearied in his self-appointed task. Although Goethe was his arch-hero, he laboured to make known to the English people other writers who were worthy of study. Reviews and essays and translations of the works of Jean Paul Richter, Musaus, Fouque, Tieck, Hoffmann, Werner, Wieland, Herder, Lessing, as well as Schiller and Goethe, came from his prolific pen, and filled the chief magazines of the day. By the force of his genius, and the persistency with which he pursued his task, he compelled English people to listen to him. His translation of "Wilhelm Meisters Lehrjahre," in three volumes, which were published in 1824, was a solid piece of work, and was the first introduction of this book to the English reading public. The study of Goethe and Schiller and other German writers had an enormous effect on Carlyle himself, and through him upon English thought. Like many others Carlyle was first attracted to Schiller, whose biography he wrote; but without being unfaithful to his first love he was drawn by stronger bands towards Goethe, whom he acknowledged as his master and teacher and spiritual father. Carlyle did his work so well that Goethe can never be so misunderstood again in England. All subsequent writers on Goethe—Matthew Arnold, Emerson, George Eliot, Thackeray, Tennyson, Sir J. R. Seeley etc., have acknowledged his greatness in almost unmeasured terms. A life of Goethe was written by G. H. Lewes in 1855; the most complete life in English was published in 1922 by the late Dr Hume Brown, the Historiographer-Royal of Scotland.

The Goethe Societies throughout the country—London, Edinburgh, Glasgow, etc.—though named after the great poet have not confined their activities to him. Their aim has been to make known the treasures of German literature not only of modern times but also of the middle high German period. Wolfram's " Parzival," Gottfried's " Tristan," the " Gudrun," the " Nibelungenlied," have found able translators and interpreters from among the members. One of the best histories of German literature in English is by a fellow-countryman of Carlyle, Professor Robertson of London University, formerly lecturer in English at the University of Strassburg, the city of Sebastian Brant where our story here began.

The study of theological and scientific works has also had its effect on the mind and language of English scholars. But that would take us beyond the scope of our present enquiry, which is to prepare the way for a clearer understanding of the influence at work in the literature of Germany which strongly affected Sir Walter Scott, and which he turned to such excellent account in his various writings, but especially in the Waverley novels.

All that is best from the German press (and some things that are not so good) has been speedily transferred to this country. It is difficult to believe that in Sir Walter Scott's time it was not possible to procure a German dictionary, for (before the war at least), the German classics have long formed a subject of study in the higher schools of the country.

Thus the German influence went on, till Germany's terrible crime in August 1914 turned the whole world against her.

German Influence on the Writings of Sir Walter Scott.

THE reader hardly needs to be reminded that the Germany of a hundred years ago which influenced Scott so strongly and left a permanent mark on all his writings, was not the Germany we know to-day. Prussia possessed the same aggressive spirit which she has always manifested, although her power was broken for a time by Napoleon. With the Prussia of their day neither Goethe nor Scott had any sympathy. The various kingdoms and duchies were then independent States; the people were simple in their habits, and practised the arts of peace in a quiet and honest way. Literature began to be seriously cultivated, and the despised German language to take the place of French which was then spoken at the Prussian Court. A small country town in the north, outside Prussia, became a great literary centre through the patronage of the Duke of Weimar, and the genius of Goethe, Schiller, Herder, Wieland, and others. From these writers Germany received a splendid literary impetus, which she has never been able fully to maintain. She has made vast strides in physical science, and in material prosperity generally, but has become more and more dominated by the military spirit, especially after the victory over the French in 1871 when unification of the various States was secured and the country styled an "Empire." This mushroom empire came to a tragic end in 1918, as all the world knows.

There has been no second Goethe, and not another "Faust." At the beginning of the war an influential German newspaper declared: "It would be difficult to find in

2

Germany 2000 persons whose intellects and hearts have remained faithful to the old Goethe ideals which dominated the Germany of fifty years ago."

Sir Walter Scott began his literary career by translations from the German; and throughout that long career much of his inspiration came from German sources. His translation of Brüger's "Lenore" among his earliest efforts was followed by an English translation of Goethe's "Goetz von Berlichingen," (published in 1799). He also translated a number of German ballads by Goethe, Herder, and others, and contributed articles on German subjects to the magazines; notably one on Hoffmann, to the "Foreign Review" in 1828, four years before his death, which attracted Goethe's attention. The same number of the "Review" contained two other articles dealing with German literature; and Carlyle pointed out to Goethe, as an evidence of the increased interest in German literature, that they were all by different authors, and none of them by himself.

It is the purpose of these pages to trace the influence of German literature on the work of Sir Walter Scott, both in his poetry, and in his novels. That influence has never been thoroughly investigated before, and this is the more surprising as it was a profound and abiding influence, greatly affecting the development of Scott's genius.

Scott's First Acquaintance with German.
His Translation of German Ballads and Dramas by Goethe.

IN his "Essay on Imitations of the Ancient Ballad," Scott has given a description of the state of knowledge in Edinburgh regarding German literature when he was a young man. A part of this essay is worth re-producing, if only to show the extraordinary change that has taken place since then. When we think of the condition of Germany and its literature in Scott's time and the prominent position that country occupied in 1914, we begin to realise what vast strides Germany had made in the interval. When we consider, also, how abundant and excellent the facilities are for acquiring the language, it requires some effort of the imagination to realise the "darkness of ignorance" that prevailed in the Modern Athens of Scott's day.

"The names of Klopstock, Schiller, Lessing, and other German poets of eminence," says Scott, "were only known in Britain very imperfectly. The 'Sorrows of Werter' was the only composition that had attained any degree of popularity, and the success of that remarkable novel, notwithstanding the distinguished genius of the author, was retarded by the nature of its incidents. To the other compositions of Goethe, whose talents were destined to illuminate the age in which he flourished, the English remained strangers ; and much more so to Schiller, Bürger, and a whole cycle of foreigners of distinguished merit. The obscurity to which German literature seemed to be condemned, did not arise from want of brilliancy in the lights by which it was illuminated, but from the palpable thickness of the darkness by which they were surrounded. . . . . ”

“ It was so late as the 21st day of April, 1788, that the literary persons of Edinburgh, of whom, at that period, I am better qualified to speak than of those of Britain generally, or especially those of London, were first made aware of the existence of works of genius in a language cognate with the English, and possessed of the same manly force of expression. They learned at the same time that the taste that determined the German compositions was of a kind as nearly allied to the English as their language. Those who were accustomed from their youth to admire Milton and Shakespeare, became acquainted, I may say for the first time, with the existence of a race of poets who had the same lofty ambition to spurn the flaming boundaries of the universe, and investigate the realms of chaos and old night ; and of dramatists, who, dis-

7

claiming the pedantry of the unities, sought, at the expense of occasional improbabilities and extravagancies, to present life in scenes of wildest contrast, and all its boundless variety of character mingling, without hesitation, livelier with more serious incidents, and exchanging scenes of tragic distress as they occur in common life, with those of a comic tendency. This emancipation from the rules so servilely adhered to by the French school, and particularly by their dramatic poets, although it was attended with some disadvantages, especially the risk of extravagance and bombast, was the means of giving free scope to the genius of Goethe, Schiller, and others, which, thus relieved from shackles, was not long in soaring to the highest pitch of poetic sublimity.

"But it was not the dramatic literature alone of the Germans which was hitherto unknown to their neighbours—their fictitious narratives, their ballad poetry, and other branches, of their literature, which are not particularly apt to bear the stamp of the extravagant and the supernatural, began to occupy the attention of the British literati."

These lines show with what intense admiration Scott regarded the newly-discovered literature of Germany. Its freshness and apparent wealth was a revelation to him, and he hastened to become better acquainted with it. With a few others like-minded, he set about learning German ; and he gives an amusing description of the class under the direction of one Dr. Willich, whose patience must have been sorely tried in his efforts, not always wisely directed, to make known his mother tongue to Edinburgh students. (See Lockhart's "Life," vol. 1. p. 204.)

Scott mentions the enthusiasm with which a translation of Schiller's "Robbers" was received at this time. It was executed by his friend, Lord Woodhouselee, an Edinburgh judge, and long eminent as professor of history in the University of Edinburgh. With that, and Professor Moir's, Carlyle's, and Scott's activity in the same direction we see that the German cult was bearing fruit. One difficulty those early enthusiasts had to contend with—"German works were at that time seldom found in London for sale—in Edinburgh never!"

Scott pursued the German language keenly; and though far from being a correct scholar, he yet became a bold and daring reader and translator of various dramatic pieces from that tongue. He returns to the difficulty of procuring books to meet his growing zeal. "The worthy and excellent friend, of whom I gave a sketch many years afterwards in the person of Jonathan Oldbuck (George Constable), procured me Adelung's Dictionary, through the medium of Father Pepper, a monk of the Scottish College of Ratisbon (German Regensburg).

Other wants of the same nature were supplied by Mrs Scott of Harden, whose kindness in a similar instance I have already had occasion to acknowledge. Through this lady's connections on the continent, I obtained copies of Bürger, Schiller, Goethe, and other standard German works."

"Being thus furnished with the necessary originals, I began to translate on all sides, certainly without anything like an accurate knowledge of the language, and although the dramas of Goethe and Schiller, and others, powerfully attracted one whose early attention to the German had been arrested by Mackenzie's Dissertation, and the play of the 'Robbers,' yet the ballad poetry, in which I had made a bold essay, was still my favourite. I was yet more delighted on finding that the old English, and especially the Scottish language, were so nearly similar to the German, not in sound merely but in the turn of phrase, that they were capable

11

of being rendered line for line, with very little variation."

Perhaps the "bold essay" in ballad poetry may have special reference to his translation of "The Erl King," by Goethe, although it was not published till after his death when it appeared in Lockhart's "Life of Scott" in 1837, and was included in the complete edition of Scott's poetical works in 1841. Scott sent his translation to Miss Christian Rutherford in 1797. He says: "I send a goblin story, you see I have not altogether lost the faculty of rhyming. I assure you there is no small impudence in attempting a version of that ballad, as it has been translated by Lewis."

From a note at the head of the poem we see that Scott's knowledge of the geography of Germany was as faulty as his knowledge of the language at this time—"The Erl-King is a goblin that haunts the Black Forest in Thuringia!"—as if one should say the Trossachs were in Yorkshire!—and the direction is—"to be read by a candle particularly long in the snuff." Scott takes liberties with his text, and seems unable to imitate the simple language of Goethe's ballad, although he has been successful in reproducing its spirit.

In the following year we hear of another ballad of Goethe's which Scott translated, or rather imitated, from the fragment introduced in Goethe's "Claudina von Villa Bella," where it is sung by one of a gang of bandits to engage the attention of the family while his companions break into the castle. The ballad, after some metrical improvements by M. G. Lewis, (known as "Monk Lewis") was published in "The Tales of Wonder." In Goethe's work it is called "Der untreue Knabe." These two translations, along with a version of Goethe's "Klagegesang der edlen Frauen des Asan Agas," Scott had printed in 1799

13

under the title, "Apology for Tales of Wonder," and distributed twelve copies among his friends.

Of these translations Lockhart says :— "The reception of the two ballads had, in the meantime, been favourable, in his own circle at least. The many inaccuracies and awkwardness of rhyme and diction to which he alludes in re-publishing them towards the close of his life, did not prevent real lovers of poetry from seeing that no one but a poet could have transfused the daring imagery of the German in a style so free, bold, masculine, and full of life; but wearied, as all such readers had been, with that succession of feeble, flimsy, lackadaisical trash which followed the appearance of the Reliques by Bishop Percy, the opening of such a new vein of popular poetry as these verses revealed, would have been enough to produce lenient critics for far inferior translations. Many, as we have seen, sent forth

14

copies of the "Lenore" about the same time; and some of these might be thought better than Scott's in particular passages; but on the whole, it seems to have been felt and acknowledged by those best entitled to judge, that he deserved the palm."

It was in 1796 that Scott published his translation of "Lenore," with that of the "Wild Huntsman," also from Bürger. He owed his copy of Bürger's works to the young lady of Harden who was a daughter of Count Brühl of Martüchen, for a long time German ambassador in London.

Scott's son's first charger, by the way, was a tall and powerful animal, named "Lenore," and the novelist called his venerable Tom cat "Hinse of Hinsfeldt" from one of the German Kindermärchen. There is a picture of "Hinse of Hinsfeldt" at Abbotsford. His liking for things German is also illustrated by the curious collection of German executioners' swords at Abbotsford.

On the blade of one of these are the arms of Augsburg, and a legend which may be rendered,

Dust, when I strike, to dust : From sleepless grave, Sweet Jesu! stoop, a sin-stained soul to save.

A few of the German curios which Scott brought to Abbotsford and which are still to be seen there, may be mentioned :—

1. A German seventeenth century flint-lock pistol, the butt end inlaid with mother-of-pearl.

2. Broadsword, with brass basket hilt, the blade by J. J. Runkel, Solingen, the "Sheffield of Germany."

3. An Executioner's sword by Arnoldt Berns, Solingen, and pierced cup hilt.

4. Another, with a German inscription on either side.

5. Two German hunting-knife blades.

6. German couteau de chasse with chased brass handle.

16

7. German stiletto with four edged blade, the handle inlaid with mother-of-pearl.

8. German two-handed sword, with long double-edged blade.

9. Another, with waved edges.

10. German Helmet of the period of Henry VIII.

11. Another sixteenth century helmet.

12. German rapier, late sixteenth century.

13. German sixteenth century burgonet, with visor and beaver.

14. Fine and rare German rapier with chased double shell hilt and large swept guard.

These antiquities Sir Walter took a particular delight in showing to German visitors and to others who were interested in Germany. They would doubtless help to stimulate his imagination when dealing with his favourite themes.

Scott was also engaged in a succession of

versions from dramas of Meier and Iffand. They are all in prose, like their originals; but Scott also versified at the same time some lyrical fragments of Goethe, for example, the Morlachian ballad.

Goetz Von Berlichingen

ALL these experiments in translation were a preparation for a more serious effort, an English version of Goethe's drama of "Goetz von Berlichingen." It was an ambitious task, to which Scott by his imperfect knowledge of the language, was not qualified to do justice, as he afterwards admitted. In the choice of such a work we see the direction in which his tastes were tending. His love of romance was early developed; indeed, it may be said to have been born with him. As a child, he revelled in the romantic ballads, with their stirring tales of border feuds and forays, and now in the drama of Goetz, he who was to be afterwards known as "the author of Waverley," found something to his liking. He set about the translation with characteristic energy and speed, and so excellent was the result that it is still received as giving a very faithful reflex of the original work. It is found in the list of standard translations in Bohn's library, with Scott's errors carefully corrected. Some of the blunders he made are rather astonishing, and quite justifies what he afterwards said to Goethe on this matter.

Lewis negotiated with Bell of London for the publication of the work. The agreement seems to have been that Bell should pay 25 guineas for the copyright, and 25 more in case of a second edition, which was not called for until long after the copyright had expired. Lewis wrote to Scott: "I have made him distinctly understand that if you accept so small a sum it will be only because this is your first publication." The translation appeared with Scott's name about a month later. Thus, by means of

Goethe, Scott makes his first bow to the reading public.

In the introduction to his translation, Scott reveals his love of ancient romance. About the artistic value of Goethe's drama he does not venture to say much. He considers it an imitation of Shakespeare's manner, not as regards the style, but in the drawing of the characters, and evolving of the motive. The idea that its great popularity in Germany arose partly from national bias, he borrowed almost verbally from an essay by his friend Henry Mackenzie.

When we compare Scott's translation with the original, we see what he means by the "terrible blunders" into which he fell. It is evident that he still trusted more to his knowledge of Anglo-Saxon and Scotch for the meaning of words than to the German dictionary. For example, Brother Martin, speaking of the garden of his monastery,

21

says, "das ist nun ihr Bienenkorb," (their beehive, i.e., their field of labour), Scott identified "Bienen" with "beans," and wrote, "where they have raised beans" (Bohnen). A little further on, the same Brother remarks, "mein Kloster ist Erfurt in Sachsen." Scott thought that "Erfurt" was from "führen," and confuses "Sachsen" with "Sachen;" so he translated, "the Convent is involved in business!"

Scott confessed long years afterwards (1827) to other mistakes. In a letter to his friend, Mrs Hughes of Uppington, he says, "I remember, among other comical blunders, I gallantly translated "Glatze," a bald head, into glasses, and made a landlord's drunken customers threaten his crockery instead of his noddle."

In spite of these unwitting blunders, and the intentional omission of certain passages, and the modification of others to suit his English readers, Scott thoroughly caught and reproduced the atmosphere of the original.

Regarding the translation of Goetz, Lockhart says:—"The reader who turns to it for the first time will be no less struck than I was under similar circumstances. . . with the many points of resemblance between the tone and spirit of Goethe's delineation, and that afterwards adopted by the translator in some of the most remarkable of his original works."

It is from his correspondence with Mrs Hughes that we learn that Scott had also translated one of Schiller's dramas, which translation was never published, and of which, apparently, Lockhart had no knowledge. He writes: "When Lockhart and Sophia leave, I will send you some similar attempts never published; one I think is a fine subject, the "Fiesco" of Schiller. I remember I used to read it to sobbing and weeping audiences, and no wonder; for

23

whatever may be thought of the translation, the original is sublime. These were the works of my nonage—not quite literally, but when I was about twenty-two or twenty-three, and certainly had no hope of doing anything out of my own head."

In another letter to the same correspondent Scott again refers to "Fiesco," and gives his opinion of the value of the revival of German literature. He says: "I admire your patience in copying out old Goetz, and I am sorry I have given away or lost a translation of "Fiesco," which is, I think, a finer thing. Some others I have, made at the same time I was German mad. If you would like to see them I could easily send them up to town, but I think they are in general sad trash, and if you read ever so little German you would see how inferior they are to the original. The publication of "Goetz" was a great era, however, in German literature, and served completely to free them from the French follies of unities and decencies of the scene, and gave an impulse to their dramas which was unique of its kind : since then they have been often stark mad, but never, I think, stupid."*

The last remark probably refers to the extravagances of Kotzebue and his school —as unlike the Weimar school of dramatists as night is to day.

*(Letters and Recollections of Sir Walter Scott by Mrs Hughes, p. 224.)

German Influence on Scott's Early Poetry, especially on "The Lay of the Last Minstrel" and in "Marmion."

SCOTT'S next work was conceived in the romantic spirit, although not dramatic in form. It was the "Lay of the Last Minstrel," and was received with enthusiasm by the reading public. Its freshness, boldness of treatment, richness of colour, appealed to many; while its national and patriotic spirit made it especially welcome to Scotsmen. But there were not wanting critics, even among his own countrymen, shrewd enough to discriminate between the original and the borrowed, between the genuine and the imitated.

"In the very first rank of poetical excellence," wrote Jeffrey, "we are inclined to place the introductory and concluding lines of every canto, in which the ancient strain is suspended, and the feelings and situation of the minstrel himself described in the words of the author. The elegance and beauty of this setting, if we may call it, though entirely of modern workmanship, appears to us to be fully more worthy of admiration than the bolder relief of the antiques which it encloses, and leads us to regret that the author should have wasted, in *imitation* and antiquarian researches, so much of those powers which seem fully equal to the task of raising him an independent reputation."

It is not difficult to know whom Scott imitated; the influence of "Goetz" is clearly traceable in the poem. The "Lay" was begun in 1802 as a ballad, on the suggestion of the young and beautiful Duchess of Buccleuch, to illustrate the customs and manners which anciently prevailed on the

Borders of England and Scotland; it grew into a long poem, which was published in 1805. In spite of its outward form, and different circumstances, the poem has certain fundamental resemblances to "Goetz."

The whole story turns on the siege of a castle. Deloraine, the chief adventurer, has not, indeed, the intellectual qualities of Goetz, but like him, he remains inactive, dallying among women's affairs, while the enemies are surrounding the walls. His comrades in arms are valiant fighters for freedom, resolute against surrender. At their head stands the mistress of the castle, who in intrepidity and womanly dignity is the image of Elizabeth, the wife of Goetz. Her son, the only boy in the poem, reminds us of the boy Georg, for in spite of his youth there is nothing he likes better than spears and horses, so that veteran soldiers prophesy for him future glory in arms. But notwithstanding the courage displayed, the garrison is little by little forced to submit to terms, not, as in the case of the German play, as the outcome of a truce, but of a tournament. Scarcely was an agreement made than unexpected relief came, an echo of the assistance brought by the faithful Sickingen.

Along with these war-like circumstances, there is a love episode. The gentle daughter of the castle is in love with the enemy of the house, and like the Maria in "Goetz," she declares in a tender scene her readiness to give him her hand in order to bring about peace and friendship between the two families. But here the lover proves himself not fickle but of knightly honour, and therein differs from the faithless Weislingen; the distinction is characteristic of the German and the Scot.

In this and in some other details, we see that while the local colouring is all Scott's own, he seems to have been indebted to

Goethe for the frame-work of the story, and method of treatment; for the action is developed, not in a quiet epical flow, but in picturesque scenes and situations. The poem could be thrown into dramatic form very easily, and, indeed, was afterwards dramatised, although not by Scott himself.

Similarly, "Goetz von Berlichingen" exercised its influence on Scott's second romantic poem, "Marmion," published in 1808. The chief person who gives his name to the poem, is a kind of Weislingen, only more energetic and nobler, and less true to life, for Scott idealised his characters by throwing around them the glamour of high-souled chivalry, and thus, in contrast with Goethe, the characters lose something in reality. Marmion, like Weislingen, has faithlessly forsaken the lover who was devoted to him, and tries to secure the affections of Clare, who despises him. The first dies mysteriously, like Adelheid, in

30

"Goetz;" the latter is betrothed to another knight, who is obliged to leave for the war after a hurried blessing in the garrison chapel, precisely like Sicknigen and Maria in similar circumstances.

In Scott's poem, the battle takes place on Flodden Field (1513). Marmion fights bravely ; his helmet is seen moving in the thickest of the fight, and some of the followers watch him from a height, filled with anxiety, as Selbitz, with his men, look at Goetz ; the details in both scenes are very much alike. Finally, Marmion is wounded and dies, partly after the manner of Weislingen and partly after the manner of Goetz. He is tortured with the thought of the dear one whom he has forsaken, and imagines he sees her, as Weislingen fancies he sees the spirit of Maria, whom he had wronged. He is forsaken by all, only the second love, the greatly injured Clare, is by him in his last moments. She points out to him the results

31

of his unfaithfulness; he begs her to pray for him. On the other hand, the unconquerable spirit of the warrior is in him, as in Goetz; he raises himself, and with his last breath cries: "Victory!" as the dying Goetz, with a supreme effort and with his last breath, shouted: "Freiheit!" "Liberty!"

The echoes of Goethe's drama were sounding in Scott's ears when he penned this description. The fact does not escape Lockhart's critical eye, and he says:—"Who does not recognise in Goethe's drama the true original of the death scene of Marmion, and the storm in 'Ivanhoe'?" (Vol. I., p. 297.)

About this time Scott prepared another dramatic work in the same romantic style, "The House of Aspen," adapted from "Der heilige Vehme" of G. Wachter. It was offered to Kemble by Lewis, and it is said to have been put into rehearsal, but it was never performed, and remained unprinted until 1829. The disappointment may have led Scott to give up the idea of writing dramas, although ancient romance still exercised its power over him. This drama is, as Scott himself said, not a translation, but a rafacimento of the original, and it is curious that where he departs from his author, he borrows from Goethe's drama. To take only one example : the first part of Scene I. of the last Act is taken almost word for word from a similar scene in " Goetz," describing the sitting of the "Vehmegericht," or Secret Tribunal. " What we admire we wish to imitate," says Scott, and he was at this time at the imitation stage of his literary career. He could scarcely have had a better model than Goethe, who, by his originality, independence, and manifest genius, stood head and shoulders above the other leaders of the new romantic movement.

Scott showed the manuscript of this

33

drama in 1808 to Miss Johanna Bailie, who gave a very frank criticism of it, and makes the remark that the dry German way of writing suits a poor poet, but not a rich one. George Ellis, on the other hand, was so delighted with this Germanized play that he told Scott he spent the evening of his wedding day in reading it to his wife!

Scott afterwards spoke contemptuously of this dramatic work as we see from a letter written in 1811 to Lady Abercorn, evidently in reply to an enquiry she had made. "I do not know anything of a play of mine," he writes, " my dear friend, unless it be a sort of a half mad German tragedy which I wrote many years ago when my taste was very green, and when like the rest of the world I was taken in with the bombast of Schiller. I never set the least value upon it, and as I gave copies to one or two people who asked for them, I am not surprised it should have risen up in judgment against me, though its resurrection has been delayed so many years. I happen fortunately to have a clean copy, of which I entreat your acceptance. The story of the Invisible Tribunal on which it is founded, is probably familiar to your ladyship. A very good little German romance entitled Hermann of Unna is founded upon it, and was translated about the time I employed myself in this idle task."

The "bombast of Schiller" probably refers to "The Robbers" with which Scott as an inveterate Tory could have no sympathy, although he justly admired the genius of Schiller.

Referring to Scott's German studies, and especially to his studies of Goethe's works, Carlyle expressed his belief that they had a considerable influence in directing, if not in developing, the genius of Scott. "If genius," he said, "could be communicated like instruction, we might call this work of

Goethe's the prime cause of 'Marmion,' 'The Lady of the Lake,' with all that has followed from the same creative hand." This is doubtless exaggeration, and while it must be admitted that the German influence was great, especially at the beginning of Scott's literary career, it was chiefly to the romantic and legendary elements that he was drawn. He read and translated the ballads of Herder, Goethe, Bürger, and others; translated and imitated German dramas and romantic tales; but it was because they were in the line of his own taste which had been early formed. These studies confirmed his tastes, but did not create them.

Scott's next poetical work, "The Lady of the Lake," shows hardly any trace of Goethe's influence either in the story, in the characters, or the details, although Carlyle seems to think otherwise. This did not result from any want of admiration for the genius of Goethe, but simply because Scott was gradually discovering his own inherent strength.

Germans and Germany

SCOTT always looked forward to visiting Germany and to meet some of those writers whom he chiefly admired. "I am fond of German literature," he wrote in 1819 to Mr Morritt of Rokeby, who was anxious about Scott's health, which was not satisfactory at this time, "and should find much amusement at one of their watering places." Writing to John Richardson four years later, he says, "I envy you your German tour, and always think time may give me such an enjoyment. *Sed fugit interea fugit irrevocabile tempus.*"

When his son, Walter, went to Germany in 1822, he gave the young officer much interesting information about the country and the people, as well as good advice as to

how he ought to behave towards the Germans. He adds, "I hope you will see Baron de la F. Motte Fouqué, as I wish to know what he is like." He had a particular admiration for this writer, as will be seen from other places.

It is not surprising that Sir Walter should have visits from friends in Germany, where his genius was early recognised, and from fellow-countrymen who had visited Germany and knew the special welcome such would receive at Abbotsford. In his Journal for 1827 he records a visit from "a smart young man, Gustavus Schwab of Königsberg; he gives a flattering picture of Prussia, which is preparing for freedom. The King must keep his word, though, or the people may chance to tire of waiting." Schwab had a considerable fame as a poet, as a biographer, and editor of the works of German poets. He died in 1850.

Again Scott records that there arrived

to breakfast (23rd March, 1829) "one of the Courland nobility, Baron A. Von Megersdorff, a fine lively spirited young man, fond of his country and incensed at its degradation under Russia. If he report correctly, there is a deep principle of action at work in Germany, Poland, Russia, etc., which if it does not die in thinking will one day make an explosion. The Germans are a nation, however, apt to exhaust themselves in speculation. The Baron has enthusiasm, and is well read in English and foreign literature."

Scott also records a visit from "a German or Hungarian, Count Erdody, or some such name."

But the most interesting German that Sir Walter encountered seems to have been Baron Münchausen, of whom he gives a detailed account in a letter to the poet Southey (26th November, 1812). "Of Baron Münchausen, I can tell you something.

40

Some years ago in London I was a little startled at hearing a foreigner ushered under this title into a musical party. As this naturally led to enquiries on my part, I was referred to the gentleman himself, who very good-humouredly told me he was the nephew of the celebrated Baron Münchausen who was a minister under Frederick of Prussia. It seems the old Baron was a humourist, who after dinner, especially if he happened to have any guests who were likely to be taken in by his marvels, used to amuse himself by inventing or retailing such marvellous adventures as are contained in the volumes which bear his name. He added, his uncle was in other respects a sensible, veracious man, and that his adventures were only told by way of quizzing or amusing society. A starving German literatus, whose name I have forgot [Rudolf Erich Raspe] who knew the Baron and thought he had been neglected by him, compiled the book in revenge, partly from the stories of the Baron, partly from other sources, and partly from his mother wit.

It proved a good hit for the bookseller, as the Baron's name and humour was well known, and by degrees made its way into other countries as a book of entertainment. The Baron Münchausen whom I knew was a grave, serious sort of a person, a good deal embarrassed by a title which required eternal explanations, and only remarkable for the zeal with which he kept grinding musical glasses the whole evening." [I. 264.]

In a letter to his friend, Daniel Terry, the actor, he relates (28th September, 1819) the following interesting circumstance: "The other day a learned American (an uncommon animal also) told me of a collection of Spanish ballads published in Germany, which interested me very much. I looked through all catalogues for it in vain, when

42

behold, young Constable just returned from Germany comes out to pay me a visit with the book in his pocket which I was hunting for, designed as a present for me!"

The learned American was George Ticknor (1791—1871), the historian of Spanish literature, and the book of ballads was Depping's "Sammlung," which is still at Abbotsford.

Scott was often visited by Lord Francis Leveson Gower, a translator of "Faust," and other German poetry in which Scott was interested, but he complains of the increasing number of foreigners that haunted Abbotsford, whose manners were often far from satisfactory. He was suffering the penalty of Continental fame, which he did not altogether appreciate when manifested in this way, but he was always a patient and courteous host.

Scott's German Secretary, Heinrich Weber
Scott's Interest in German Romances and Translations from These

SIR Walter Scott kept a German in his employment for ten years, Heinrich, or Henry Weber, who had been sent down to Ashiestiel by some of the London booksellers in a half-starved condition. He acted as amanuensis and secretary to Scott, and was very serviceable to him in many ways. Scott had great faith in his abilities, and actually encouraged him in editing for the press an edition of Beaumont and Fletcher's works. He placed at Weber's disposal his own annotated copy, but the result was a complete failure, and Lockhart expressed his amazement that Scott

should ever have countenanced the project
of an edition of an English book of this class,
by a mere drudging German although he
admits that Weber was a man of considerable learning. Weber relieved Scott of a
good deal of drudgery, especially in the way
of copying and making extracts from German sources which were turned to account
by Scott in the third edition of "Sir
Tristrem." Weber's demeanour was gentle
and modest, and, avows Lockhart, he had
not only a stock of curious antiquarian
knowledge, but reminiscences which he
detailed with the amusing simplicity of an
early life chequered with many strange
adventures.

This German was treated more as a friend
of the family than as a servant, the more so
as Scott noticed that he had an unhappy
propensity to drinking, which grew upon
him, and was finally his ruin. In one of his
lapses he suddenly challenged his master

to a duel with pistols while they were in the library together at Abbotsford. Scott, with great adroitness and presence of mind, relieved the man of the weapons, and secretly sent for assistance, but it was found necessary to remove the poor fellow to an asylum. He was supported there to the end of his life, the next four years, at Scott's expense. Sir Walter, who missed his services very much, pays him a generous compliment, testifying that Weber, ''besides possessing a very extensive general acquaintance with literature, was particularly deep in our old dramatic lore, a good modern linguist, a tolerable draughtsman and antiquary and a most excellent hydrographer.''

The last of Weber's literary productions were the analysis of the old German poems of the "Helden Buch," and the "Nibelungen Lied," published in 1814, in which Scott had a large share. The rhymed versions of the '' Nibelungen Lied '' were from Scott's

GOETHE, FROM THE PAINTING BY HEINRICH KOLBE, 1826.

facile pen, and he contributed to the collection an account of the "Eyrbiggia Saga." These old German legends and sagas had an endless charm for Sir Walter Scott. (See Kenilworth, chap. VIII.)

Scott's confidence in his skill in verse translation is further illustrated by the offer which he made to a Scotch friend, G. Huntly Gordon, whom he wished to assist. He arranged that Gordon should translate a German novel, "The Travels of Thiodolf," by Motte Fouqué. He gives Gordon some advice as to the principles of translation, which he himself had followed, and adds with regard to the poems that occur in the novel : "If you find the versification a difficult or unpleasant task, I must translate for you such parts of the poetry as may be absolutely necessary for carrying on the story, which will cost an old hack like me very little trouble."

The ease and readiness with which Scott

could turn a German ballad into English is also illustrated by the following anecdote related by Lockhart :—

" While walking about before dinner with his dear friend·Mr Skene of Rubislaw who had lived many years in Germany and knew the language and the literature well, Skene recited the German " Kriegslied," or war song, " Der Abschieds Tag ist da " (the Day of Departure has come "). It delighted both Scott and Lewis who was present. Next morning Scott produced that spirited little piece in the same measure, which, embodying the volunteer ardour of the time, was forthwith adopted as the troop song of the Edinburgh light horse."

While Scott was busy with novel writing he was, at the same time interesting himself in the translation of works from the German, and looking about for a suitable translator. His own hands were full, and he expressed himself as fearing that a mere "literal jog-trotter" like himself was not fit for the task. In writing on the subject to his friend Daniel Terry, who seems to have started the proposal, he says : "Unquestionably I know many interesting works of the kind, which might be translated from the German : — almost all those of Musaeus, of which Beddoes made two volumes, and which are admirably written ; many of La Motte Fouqué; several from the collection of Beit Weber. But there is a point more essential to their success with the British public than even the selection. There is in the German mode of narration an affection of deep metaphysical reflection and protracted description and discussion, which the English do not easily tolerate ; and whoever translates their narratives with effect should be master of the task and spirit of both nations. For instance, I lately saw a translation of "Sintram und seine Gefährten," or "Sintram and his

Comrades," "Sintram" is by La Motte Fouqué, the story of the world which, if the plot were insinuated into the "boxes," as Bayes says, would be most striking, translated into such English as was far more difficult to me than the original German."

It will be seen from these lines that Scott was still keeping himself in touch with contemporary German literature. He refers also to this in the introduction to "Guy Mannering."

James Skene of Rubislaw.

IN tracing German influence on Sir Walter
Scott we must not omit to mention the
share which a fellow-countryman had
in encouraging and strengthening his in-
clinations. Sir Walter, who eagerly seized
every opportunity of extending his knowledge of the language and literature of
Germany, was very glad to make the
acquaintance of a young man, James Skene
of Rubislaw, who had just returned from a
residence in that country. Skene had an
excellent collection of German books ; and
of these Scott made ample use. The
acquaintance ripened into a friendship which
lasted from 1794 to Scott's death in 1832.
During that long period Skene was a never
failing help and stimulus, and was of especial

assistance with some of the novels, notably,
" Guy Mannering," " Ivanhoe," " Quentin
Durward," and " Anne of Geierstein."

Skene's own account of their friendship
deserves to be quoted for the further light
it throws on Scott's literary development
through the influence of his early and later
German studies.

" My first acquaintance with Sir Walter
Scott," says Skene, " arose from the circumstance of my having at an early period
of my life acquired some knowledge of the
German language, and having thus anticipated the time when a taste for it began
to gain ground in this country. Until the
close of the last century the literature of
Germany was but little known in Scotland,
where the idea prevailed that it contained
few treasures worth knowing, and that it
was chiefly confined to monkish chronicles,
and such like dry annals of the numerous
small states and dependencies into which

the country was sub-divided, with ponderous tomes of commentators on Law, Theology, and the Classics, and treatises on Alchemy and the Occult Sciences. But about this time the first works of Schiller and Klopstock had begun to be noticed, and some of the wild ballads, or " Volkslieder " of Bürger, having fallen into Scott's hands, he forthwith set himself to work to master the idiom, and even to translate some of them into English. The chivalrous and romantic character of most of these legendary tales chimed in with the bent and task of Sir Walter's mind, and having somewhat familiarised himself with the structure of the language by putting the play of "Goetz von Berlichingen " into an English dress, he made a very successful translation of " Leonore," and some of the other ballads. Books of this class, however, were but rarely to be met with in the country at that period, and in his quest for a supply to feed the craving for German romance that seized him, Sir Walter learned that I had recently returned from a several years' residence at school in Germany, and that I had brought a collection of the best German authors along with me, which he, of course, became desirous to obtain access to. However, the objects of his research were there before him in a goodly range of German volumes, comprehending the works of most of the German authors then in repute ; they soon fixed his attention, and became the subject of our conversation, and when I intimated to him that the collection was altogether at his service, a cordial shake of the hand which accompanied his thanks seemed to seal that bond, which rose from this first introduction to an intimacy and friendship uninterrupted for forty years, and even still on the increase when the close of his life dissolved that bond of affection which had constituted one of the chief charms of mine."

(Memories of Sir Walter Scott by James Skene ; edited by Basil Thomson, 1909 (p. 4.)

Scott's skill in translating from German to English was once made by him the touchstone or test of returning health after a severe illness. The story is told by Skene:—

" In the progress of his illness upon this occasion he asked me one day to read to him a short ballad of Bürger in German, that he might amuse himself in translating, which was accordingly done, and he put up the translation in his pocket book, and refused to let me see it, saying it was not worth reading. However, some months after, when he began to be decidedly convalescent, he reminded me of the translation, and taking it out of his pocket-book, he said that he had had his reasons both for writing it and for refusing to show what he had written, and that he now felt more nervous than he could express in putting it to the use he intended, which was as a test of the state of his mind during his late illness, for that he had had frequent misgivings in the progress of it that his faculties were giving way, and might never again be recovered. 'Now, I really am not bold enough,' he said, 'to be my own executioner; do you now take the manuscript, and after I have read the original, read it aloud, and let it pronounce the sentence of sanity or imbecility as it may chance.' Accordingly this singular experiment was put to the test. Sir Walter read his part, and turning his head aside, desired me to go on, and upon my reading the translation, which really was very good, cast a most whimsical glance from under his heavy eyebrows, 'Well, is Richard himself again?' There was no doubt of it. I wanted to pocket the manuscript, but he would not suffer me; he said it had answered its end and must not be urged further." ("Memories of Scott," p. 70.)

James Skene died at Frewen Hall, near Oxford, in 1864, in his ninetieth year, thus outliving his friend by thirty-two years. Very early in their friendship (1808) Scott had expressed his appreciation of Skene by dedicating the introduction of Canto IV. in "Marmion" to him. Scott was the Quarter-Master, and Skene Cornet, in the Royal Edinburgh Light Horse Volunteers.

German Influence on Scott's Novels

THUS far we have seen something of the influence that German literature exercised upon Scott in the early part of his career, first as a translator, and then as a poet. We have only indirectly referred to this influence in some of his novels. We now propose going into this subject more in detail. There are thirteen out of the twenty-five romances where German influence is most distinctly traceable, and these we shall take in the order of their publication.

Guy Mannering (1815).

Guy Mannering was the first romance that appeared after "Waverley," which gave its name to the series. Scott himself

described it as "a tale of private life, and
only varied by the perilous exploits of
smugglers and excisemen," and was "the
work of six weeks at a Christmas." It was
received by the public with even greater
enthusiasm than "Waverley." It was put
into dramatic form in 1816 by Scott's
friend Daniel Terry, the actor, and met
with great success on the London boards.
Scott took a personal interest in this work
of "Terry-fying," as he called it, and supplied the pretty song of the "Lullaby."

One would hardly look for evidence of
German influence in a Scotch novel, especially with the chief hero an Englishman, who
also gives the title to the story. But when
Scott wrote "Guy Mannering" the German influence was still potent with him,
and comes out in the character of Dirk
Hatteraick. This famous smuggler, it is
true, is represented as a Dutchman, but he
is more German than Dutch, in speech at

least. Dirk Hatteraick could swear in Dutch, German, and English, the author tells us, but Scott's familiarity with High German makes the smuggler use it rather than Dutch, or Low German; and the bacchanalian song which Dirk sings to Glossin is High German, or as Scott calls it, High Dutch (Hoch Deutsch.)

Take, as an example of Hatteraick's speech, the following :—

"What bin I? Donner and blitzen! I bin Jans Janson, from Cuxhaven (in Germany) what sall ich bin?"

"Es spuckt da!"

"Strafe mich hélle!"

"Hagel and donner! be'st du?"

"Hold mich der deyvil, Ich bin ganz gefrorne!"

"Das schmeckt!" he exclaims, as he tastes the spirits. Then he breaks out into the fragment of a German drinking song, which we might be inclined to think Scott had found in some German student's song book; for it is still sung at the University "Kneipe."

Saufen Bier, und Brantewein,
Schmeissen alle die Fenstern ein,
Ich bin liederlich,
Du bist liederlich,
Sind wir nicht liederlich Leute?

But the matter is put beyond doubt by what Skene tells us in his "Memories of Sir Walter Scott." (p. 52).

"Something," says Skene, "in the course of one of our rides had suggested to me the words of a German drinking song, which I repeated to him; it took his fancy, and he made me repeat it to him two or three times over, which led me to expect a translation; and accordingly my song very soon made its appearance, not in translation, but "in ipsissimis verbis," as Dirk Hatteraick's song in "Guy Mannering." Scott gives a very "free" version of the song in English.

Let the reader who knows German follow Dirk Hatteraick's further talk, and he will be convinced that Scott has presented us with a life-like portrait of a jolly, beer-drinking German.

"The Antiquary" (1816)

"THE Antiquary" was Scott's favourite novel. One can see that he bestowed infinite pains on its composition. In the portrayal of the characters we have also evidence of much careful study. For our present purpose it is only necessary to note that the leading character who gives his name to the romance is presented to us as being of German descent. In Mr Jonathan Oldbuck, Scott confesses that he was seeking to portray his friend George Constable; but strangely enough, he gives him a German origin and a German name. The first Oldenbuck was descended from one of the original printers of Germany, and had left his country owing to the persecutions that followed the Reformation.

Mr Jonathan was proud of his ancestry, although, when he and Sir Arthur Wardour chanced to fall out, the latter would declare to his daughter that Oldbuck had still something of the German boorishness flowing in his veins ; while Oldenbuck would aver that Sir Arthur was cherishing dreams of standing armies and German oppression. All this sounds quite modern and up to date.

The two friends, notwithstanding a certain attachment and respect for each other, seldom parted without a quarrel over some antiquarian subject. Very plain language was used on those occasions by both controversialists. Sir Arthur is defending Henry Maule of Melgum not only as an antiquarian authority but as " a gentleman of high family and ancient descent," and therefore—

" The descendant of a Westphalian printer should speak of him with deference. I conceive that my descent from that

64

painful (painstaking) and industrious typographer, Wolfbrand Oldenbuck, who in the month of December 1493, under the patronage, as the colophon says, of Sebaldus Scheyter and Sebastian Kammermeister, accomplished the printing of the great "Chronicle of Nuremberg. I conceive, I say, that my descent from that great restorer of learning is more creditable to me as a man of letters than if I had numbered in my genealogy all the brawling, bulletheaded, iron-fisted old Gothic barons since the days of Crenthemīnacheryme, not one of whom, I suppose, could write his own name." (Chap. vi.)

Oldenbuck never loses an opportunity of extolling the greatness of his German ancestor. When the subject of the haunted room comes up in Oldenbuck's house where young Lovel was to sleep, he says, "There was always some idle story of the room being haunted by the spirit of Aldobrand

65

Oldenbuck, my great-great-great-grand-father. He was a foreigner, and wore his national dress, of which tradition had preserved an accurate description ; and indeed there is a print of him, supposed to be by Reginald Elstracke, pulling the press with his own hand, as it works off the sheets of his scarce edition of the Augsburg Confession. He was a chemist as well as a good mechanic, and either of these qualities in this country was at that time sufficient to constitute a white witch at least."

"Why, Grizel," he continued when interrupted, "the doctor is a good honest, pudding-headed German, of much merit in his own way, but fond of the mystical, like many of his countrymen."

Then the Antiquary led his guest to the haunted chamber, lighting his way with a candle fixed on a candlestick of massive silver and antique form, which, he observed, was wrought out of the silver found in the

mines of the Harz Mountains, and had been
the property of the very personage who had
supplied them with a subject of conversation. Next morning the Antiquary
brings forth the famous work of his ancestor.
"There, Mr Lovel," he exclaimed, "there
is the work I mentioned to you last night—
the rare quarto of the Augsburg Confession,
the foundation at once and the bulwark of
the Reformation, drawn up by the learned
and venerable Melancthon, defended by the
Elector of Saxony and the other valiant
hearts who stood up for their faith even
against the front of a powerful and victorious emperor, and imprinted by the scarcely
less venerable and praise-worthy Aldobrand
Oldenbuck, my happy progenitor, during
the yet more tyrannical attempts of Philip
II. to suppress at once civil and religious
liberty. Yes, sir, for printing this work that
eminent man was expelled from his ungrate-
ful country, and driven to establish his

household gods even here at Monkbarns, among the ruins of papal superstition and domination.

"Read, I say, his motto, for each printer had his motto or device when that illustrious art was first practised. My ancestor's was expressed, as you see, in the Teutonic phrase, "Kunst macht Gunst"; that is, skill or prudence in availing ourselves of our natural talents and advantages will compel favour and patronage, even where it is withheld from prejudice or ignorance." "And that," said Lovel after a moment's thoughtful silence—"that then is the meaning of these German words."

"Unquestionably; you perceive the appropriate application to a consciousness of inward worth, and of eminence in a useful and honourable art. Each printer in those days, as I have already informed you, had his device, his impress as I may call it, in the same manner as the doughty chivalry of the age, who frequented tilt and tournament. My ancestor boasted as much in his as if he had displayed it over a conquered field of battle, though it betokened the diffusion of knowledge, not the effusion of blood. And yet there is a family tradition which affirms him to have chosen it from a more romantic circumstance."

Lovel desires to know what that circumstance was, and it may be quoted here to show Scott's familiarity with a good custom that once prevailed in Germany, and continued in some parts of the country down to Scott's day and even later. Goethe has immortalised the custom in Wilhelm Meister's "Wanderjahre" which was translated into English, and published in Edinburgh in 1827.

"It is said my ancestor," continues the Antiquary, "during his apprenticeship with the descendant of old Fust, whom popular tradition hath sent to the devil under the name of Faustus, was attracted by a paltry slip of womankind, his master's daughter, called Bertha. They broke rings, [an ancient German custom] or went through some idiotical ceremony, as is usual on such idle occasions as the plighting of a true-love troth, and Aldobrand set out on his journey through Germany as became an honest "handworker"; for such was the custom of mechanics at that time, to make a tour through the Empire, and work at their trade for a time in each of the most eminent towns before they finally settled themselves for life. It was a wise custom; for, as such travellers were received like brethren in each town by those of their own handicraft, they were sure in every case to have the means either of gaining or communicating knowledge. When my ancestor returned to Nuremburgh (Nürnberg) he is said to have found his old master newly dead, and two or three gallant young suitors, some of them half-starved sprigs of nobility forsooth, in pursuit of the jungfrau Bertha, whose father was understood to have bequeathed her a dowry which might weigh against sixteen armorial quarters. But Bertha, not a bad sample of womankind, had made a vow she would only marry that man who could work her father's press. The skill at that time was as rare as wonderful; besides, that the expedient rid her at once of most of her 'gentle' suitors, who would have as soon wielded a conjuring wand as a composing stick. Some of the more ordinary typographers made the attempt, but none were sufficiently possessed of the mystery.

"However, Aldobrand arrived in the ordinary dress, as we would say, of a journeyman printer—the same in which he had traversed Germany, and conversed with Luther, Melancthon, Erasmus, and other learned men, who disdained not his know-

ledge, and the power he possessed of diffus-
ing it, though hid under a garb so homely.
But what appeared so respectable in the
eyes of wisdom, religion, learning, and
philosophy seemed mean, as might readily
be supposed, and disgusting in those of silly
and affected womankind, and Bertha refused to acknowledge her former lover in
the torn doublet, skin cap, clouted shoes,
and leathern apron of a travelling handi-
craftsman or mechanic. He claimed his
privilege, however, of being admitted to a
trial ; and when the rest of the suitors had
either declined the contest, or made such
work as the devil could not read if his par-
don depended on it, all eyes were bent on
the stranger. Aldobrand stepped graceful-
ly forward, arranged the types without
omission of a single letter, hyphen, or
comma, imposed them without deranging a
single space, and pulled off the first proof
as clean and free from errors as if it had been

a triple revise! All applauded the worthy successor of the immortal Faustus, the blushing young maiden acknowledged her error in trusting to the eye more than the intellect, and the elected bridegroom thence forward chose for his impress or device the appropriate words, "Skill wins favour." ("Kunst macht Gunst.")"

In this character Scott delineates a German of the fine old fashioned type, with his simple dignity, love of learning, and perfect honesty. He was a stout Protestant and proud of his religion as of his ancestry. He resents with indignation the insinuation of Lord Glenallan that a Protestant could not be trusted. "I should hope, my lord," said Oldbuck gravely, "that a Protestant may be as trustworthy as a Catholic. I am doubly interested in the Protestant faith, my lord. My ancestor, Aldobrand Olden-buck, printed the celebrated Confession of

Augsburg, as I can show by the original edition now in this house."

At the end of the story we are told that when Lord Geraldin was married to Miss Wardour, the Antiquary made the lady a present of the wedding ring, a massy circle of antique chasing, bearing the motto of Aldobrand Oldenbuck, "Kunst macht Gunst."

There is another German character introduced into this novel. He is altogether different from the other, but is also typical of a certain class of Germans largely represented at the present day. This is the notorious Hermann Dousterswivel, a man who was as unscrupulous as he was clever and cunning. He practised his cunning upon the impecunious knight, Sir Arthur Wardour, with the promise of discovering a vein of gold on the estate, which would restore the knight's shattered fortunes. This Dousterswivel is made to speak a kind of broken English with an admixture of German words ; and Scott is here probably imitating the style of speech of his servant and secretary, Weber. Dousterswivel liked to remind Mr Oldbuck that he is a fellow countryman, although the latter did not appreciate the honour and did not hide his opinion that Dousterswivel was an "impudent knave." The trick of pretending to find water by means of a magic wand was the preliminary to further acts of deception practised upon Sir Arthur, but which could not impose upon the shrewd old Antiquary.

It was to the pic-nic party in the wood that Miss Wardour read one of those German legends that were so common in the eighteenth century ;—the scene being laid among the Harz mountains, more especially on that called the Brocken, chosen haunt of witches, demons, and apparitions of all kinds. "Miss Wardour had made it just like one romance," Dousterswivel said, "as well as Goethe, or Wieland, could have done it, by mine honest wort."

The story is too long to repeat here. The reader who feels interested in it will find it at Chapter 18 of the "Antiquary," it is called "The Fortunes of Martin Waldeck." Scott says it is taken from the German, although he is "unable to say in which of the various collections of the popular legends in that language the original is to be found." It illustrates Scott's familiarity with German legendary lore, and the translation is of course his own. Why Scott should intrude this German story into a Scotch novel is not very clear, except that it had fascinated himself. There are countless legends and romantic stories connected with the Harz mountains. How Scott would have delighted, had it been his good fortune, to make a walking tour over those mountains, as so many of his countrymen have done, to get first hand acquaintance

with their legends! Those who have walked
through that enchanted land will never
forget it, and Scott's German visitors at
Abbotsford must have sometimes spoken of
its charm.

> Goethe too had been there,
> In the long-past winter he came
> To the frozen Harz, with his soul
> Passionate, eager—his youth
> All in ferment.
>
> (Matthew Arnold.)

To return to Dousterswivel. The midnight scene in which he and Sir Arthur
Wardour at the instigation of the former
seek for the treasured gold in the cavern is
graphically described and not without some
humour, especially when the unexpected
sneeze of Edie Ochiltree alarms both
searchers, and the knight exclaims, "Lord
have mercy on us!" and the German invo-
luntarily using his mother tongue cries,
"Alle guten Geistern loben den Herrn!"
Scott never conceals his contempt for this

German, and paints him as an out and out villain without one redeeming feature in his character. All those who have dealings with him, even Sir Arthur Wardour, distrust him. Dousterswivel is little troubled with qualms of conscience, although he shares the superstition of his countrymen when they have thrown off the restraints of religion. This "scoundrelly German"; as the Antiquary rightly calls him, meets with a fate that is really too good for him, he is banished—"sent back to play the knave in his own country."

There is an amusing story in Chapter IV. of the "Antiquary," which, since it was related, has been held up as a warning to over learned gentlemen, especially antiquaries.

Old Monkbarns brings his friends to what he describes with much detail and argument as the site of a Roman camp, where according to the imaginative antiquary,

"Julius Agricola beheld what our Beaumont has so admirably described : From this very Praetorium."

A voice from behind interrupted his ecstatic description — "Praetorian here, Praetorian there, I mind the bigging o't."

Now, a very similar story is related in a German work which was published in 1803. It is "Spaziergang nach Syrakus," by Johann Gottfried Seume (1763-1810). The author was a friend of Crabb Robinson and together they made a pilgrimage to Weimar to visit Goethe. Seume was a scholar and a lover of books, but also a traveller, and this book is an account of his visit to Syracuse in Sicily. During his stay there he became acquainted with an Italian scholar whose tastes were like his own, and who related to him an anecdote of his being on an archaeological expedition with some Germans about the depression cut upon a rock. Various theories were propounded, one that it was the grave of some child of noble birth. During the dispute a peasant drew near and offered an explanation less romantic. "About twenty years ago," he said, "I cut out the hole myself to make a feeding trough for my swine. But for some years I have not kept swine, and so I do not feed them out of it."

Had Scott read this German work and was it the source of the anecdote in the "Antiquary" published in 1816? We would be inclined to think so from what we know of Scott's borrowings from German sources, especially at a time when he seems to have been so strongly under German influence; of this we have abundant evidence in the "Antiquary."

Lockhart, however, says: "William Clerk well remembers his father telling a story which was introduced in due time in the "Antiquary." While he was visiting his grandfather, Sir John Clerk, at Dumcrieff, in Dumfries-shire, many years before this time, the old Baronet carried some English virtuosos to see a supposed Roman camp ; and on his exclaiming at a particular spot, ' This I take to have been the Praetorium,' a herdsman, who stood by, answered, 'Praetorium here Praetorium there, I made it with a flaughter spade.' "

Let the reader himself decide the point as to the origin of this historic anecdote with the evidence he has before him.   We simply record the facts, but it should be remembered that Lockhart was not above doing a little " embellishing " where the facts seemed to call for it, and that the enthusiasm of the elder Clerk for antiquities " was often played on " by his young relatives by means of artificial " antiquities."   Is it improbable that Scott, finding the story in Seume, communicated it to the elder Clerk who retailed it to his son, giving it at the same time a "local habitation and a name?"

It is an interesting point, though not of infinite importance.

The Legend of Montrose (1819)

THIS is another of the Scotch novels in which it might seem useless to look for any trace of Sir Walter Scott's German partialities ; yet even here he manages to introduce, if not a German character, one who had served in German wars, and could therefore give opportunities of bringing in German speech and German peculiarities.

This character is the famous Sir Dugald Dalgetty. He describes himself to Lord Menteith in the following words : "My name is Dalgetty—Dugald Dalgetty, Ritt-Master, Dugald Dalgetty of Drumthwacket, at your honourable service to command. It is a name you may have seen in "Gallo

Belgicus," the "Swedish Intelligencer," or, if you read High Dutch, (German), in the "Fliegenden Mercoeur" of Leipsic. My father, my lord, having by unthrifty courses reduced a fair patrimony to a nonentity, I had no better shift, when I was eighteen years auld than to carry the learning whilk I had acquired at the Mareschal College of Aberdeen, my gentle bluid and designation of Drumthwacket, together with a pair of stalwarth arms, and legs conform, to the German wars, there to push my way as a cavalier of fortune."

He continues : "Surely, my lord, it doth not become me to speak ; but he that hath seen the field of Leipsic and of Lützen, may be said to have seen pitched battles. And one who hath witnessed the intaking of Frankfort, and Spanheim, and Nuremberg, and so forth, should know somewhat about leaguers, storms, onslaughts, and outfalls. I was ultimately promoted to be a fahndragger, as the High Dutch call it (which signifies an ancient) in the King's Leif Regiment of Black Horse, and thereafter I rose to be lieutenant and ritt-master, under that invincible monarch, the bulwark of the Protestant faith, the Lion of the North, the terror of Austria, Gustavus the Victorious."

By the questions of Lord Menteith we get many particulars regarding the ways and manners of the soldiers. Dalgetty compares favourably, of course, the Scotch with the Germans. "I have seen whole regiments," he says, "of Dutch and Holsteiners meeting on the field of battle like base scullions, crying out "Gelt, Gelt," (money, money), signifying their desire of pay, instead of falling to blows like our noble Scottish blades, who ever disdained, my lord, postponing of honour to filthy lucre."

Scott here and elsewhere makes good use of his chance to display his knowledge of German military customs. We hear much through Dalgetty about Tilly and the renowned Wallenstein. Schiller made Wallenstein the subject of three dramas, published in 1800, with which Scott, as we shall see, was familiar.

The close intercourse of the Scotch with Germany in the sixteenth and seventeenth centuries is well brought out in this delightful character of Sir Dugald. The causes that led to that close connection were chiefly military and religious. There were many Scottish soldiers of fortune who were urged by love of adventure rather than by uncertain pay to give their services on the Continent, while others were driven by stress of poverty or religious persecution at home. Many such never returned to their native country. It will be remembered that the grandfather of the celebrated philosopher, Immanuel Kant, was a Scotsman, who had settled in the north of Germany, and was saddler by trade. The philosopher changed

the spelling of the name from " Cant " to
" Kant."

Dugald Dalgetty seems to have wandered
all over Germany in service of various kinds;
not only is he found at Frankfort-on-Main,
(afterwards famed as Goethe's birthplace),
but also at Frankfort-on-Oder in the north,
and further north still at Rostock in Meck-
lenburg, on the shores of the Baltic. But he
is always true to the instincts of his native
land ; he never forgets what he owes to his
" alma mater," the Mareschal College of
Aberdeen ; he likes to know before hand
what remuneration he is to receive for his
services, and from what funds it is to be
paid, although, with admirable inconsis-
tency, he condemns the same prudence in
others—" I hold it a mean and sordid thing
for a " soldado " to have nothing in his
mouth but pay and " gelt," like the base
scullions, the German " lanzknechts."

He mentions a curious weapon used by

the Germans and called by them "Morgen-stern" (morning star), which Scott in a foot-note explains as "a sort of club, or mace, used in the earlier part of the seventeenth century in the defence of breaches and walls. When the Germans insulted a Scotch regi-ment then besieged in Trailsund, saying they heard there was a ship come from Denmark to them laden with tobacco pipes, 'One of our soldiers,' says Colonel Robert Munro, 'showing them over the work of a "morgenstern," made of a large stock banded with iron, like the shaft of a halberd, with a round globe at the end with cross iron pikes,' saith, 'Here is one of the tobacco pipes wherewith we will beat out your brains when you intend to storm us.'"

Whe. Dalgetty tucks himself up in bed he repeats "the first verse of the Lutheran psalm, 'Alle guter geister loben den Herrn.'" On another occasion he uses the same words as an exorcism, but gives the German more correctly—"'alle guten geister loben, den Herrn," saith the blessed Psalmist, in Dr. Luther's translation." Scott had a good working knowledge of German and French, as well as Spanish and Italian, but he was not an accurate scholar in any of those languages.

When Captain Dalgetty saw the defences of Sir Duncan Campbell's Castle, he protested to God that they reminded him more of the notable fortress of Spandau (near Berlin) situated in the march of Brandenburg, than of any place whilk it had been his fortune to defend in the course of his travels.

When he is brought into the presence of the Marquis of Argyle, he defends himself nobly, declaring that he can refer his lordship to the invincible Gustavus Adolphus, the Lion of the North, to Bannier, Oxenstiern, to the warlike Duke of Saxe-Weimar,

Tilly, Wallenstein, Piccolomini, and other great captains, both dead and living.

The author makes this valiant Scotsman say, "Lecture or homily, it was as the High Germans say, 'ganz fortre flich,'" a phrase whose meaning we can only guess, for it is not real German.

Dalgetty hears the sullen toll of a large bell, and exclaims, "That must be the alarm—the storm-clock, as the Germans call it (Sturmglocken)."

He recalls the famous battle of Lützen when his never-to-be-forgotten master told Francis Albert, Duke of Saxe-Lauenburg, to shift for himself; and he declares that he himself was in as great pinches in Germany, more especially at the fatal battle of Nerlingen. He remembers how, in the streets of Nuremberg, the people would have almost worshipped his master, and he quotes an example of strict discipline at the field of Leipzig, a lesson whilk is not to be forgotten.

Scott takes the opportunity of explaining in a footnote that in German, as in Latin, the original meaning of the word Ritter, corresponding to Eques, is merely a horseman.

To judge by the boasting of the valiant Scottish knight, he had seen service in every part of Germany, from Rostock to Ingolstadt. When Ranald MacEagh was dying, he asked Dugald, "Hadst thou ever an enemy against whom weapons were of no avail?" "Very frequently when I served in Germany," replied Sir Dugald. "There was such a fellow at Ingolstadt, he was proof against lead and steel. The soldiers killed him with the butts of their muskets."

"The Legend of Montrose" is connected with the civil war between Charles I. and his Parliament about the year 1645. The localities in which the chief events of the story lie are in various parts of Scotland; and all the characters, without exception,

91

are Scotch. It is the more remarkable, therefore, that such a strong German element should appear, and that, by means of a Scotsman, the delightful and original Captain Dugald of Drumthwacket. It illustrates, surely, the author's German leanings, but no one will complain about the manner in which he has turned to account his knowledge of the language and the people. The events described, or rather hinted at, as having taken place in contemporary Germany, form an off-set and back-ground to the events more fully detailed as taking place in Scotland when "fair women and brave men" did doughty deeds for the cause which they had espoused.

Ivanhoe (1819)

WHEN Scott wrote "Ivanhoe," he opened a new and rich vein of romance. He had hitherto confined himself to Scotland and Scottish themes; but, fearing lest he might weary out the public favour, he determined to break new ground and deal with a subject purely English. The period dealt with was the reign of Richard I. before Saxon and Norman had commingled; and this afforded an ample field for stirring and romantic adventure. The freshness of the ground which he was now to traverse seems also to have given him new zest; and the result is one of the finest—probably the very finest—of the romances that came from his pen. He prepared himself carefully for the task; and when he began to write, threw his whole soul into the composition of the story. Page after page of unblotted and uncorrected manuscript passed directly from his hand to that of the printer with astonishing rapidity.

The subject is so thoroughly English, and the characters and situations are drawn with such a firm and bold hand, that it may be supposed we should look in vain for any trace of German influence in the story. But in one important scene, describing the seige of Torquilstone Castle by the Saxon hosts, we cannot help being reminded of a similar scene in "Götz von Berlichingen," of which Scott had already made use in "Marmion." Lockhart's trained eye detected the likeness, and in his criticism of "Ivanhoe," which he praises highly, he quotes the scene from Götz, and asks, "Who does not recognise in Goethe's drama the true original of the death scene of Marmion, and the storm in Ivanhoe?"

ABBOTSFORD HOUSE.

We know that Scott was not only an industrious reader of German romances, and especially of Goethe's writings, but also of Schiller's works so far as they came within his reach. He had read Lord Woodhouselee's translation of Schiller's "Robbers" as far back as 1792, and was stimulated to his first experiments in the same walk. Schiller was Goethe's friend ; and the two collaborated in certain literary work. He lived at Weimar, near Goethe, during the last years of his life, and died in 1805.

Scott seems to have been familiar with Schiller's drama "The Maid of Orleans," and makes apt use of a quotation from it. The chapter which describes the siege of Torquilstone Castle which is watched from a latticed window by Rebecca who reports progress to Ivanhoe, is headed by the following lines from Schiller :

Ascend the watch tower yonder, valiant soldier,
Look on the field, and say how goes the battle. (ch. 29).

It may be urged that this has not much significance, no more significance than a quotation from Shakespeare which serves for a motto to a succeeding chapter. But this is not so. There would be nothing unusual in quoting from Shakespeare ; but at that time to quote from a German author was surprising ; and this is what Scott does. The works of even the best writers were difficult to procure, and only to Scott and the few Scottish enthusiasts in German literature were they possible of access. Scott, too, must have read Schiller's drama in the original, for although "The Maid of Orleans " was published in Germany in 1802, and " Ivanhoe " in 1819, yet the earliest English translation did not appear till 1835. We may therefore suppose that this is Scott's own translation of the lines which he put as a motto to this chapter, and it gives a further and not insignificant proof of his interest in German authors, and the use to which he could turn them in a purely English story. The quotation from the "Maid" will be found in Act. v., scene 2.

One of the most beautiful figures in Scott's gallery of female characters is the Jewish Rebecca in "Ivanhoe," on whom he seems to have bestowed much loving care and study. Her pure and lofty spirit and virtuous character, invulnerable against every assault, is in itself a tribute to the author's high ideal of womanhood. We have to go to Shakespeare for anyone to equal her. Scott was jealous of her reputation and defends himself in the Introduction for leaving her high-toned virtue unrewarded by mere temporal prosperity, and not having assigned the hand of Ivanhoe to her rather than to the less interesting Rowena. She is too noble, he says in effect, to be rewarded after the manner of the world by mere wealth or earthly rank. Her own pure and noble life was her best reward, and the peace which the world cannot give or take away.

It may be surprising to learn that we owe this beautiful creation to a German source, through James Skene of Rubislaw. The Jewish scenes in "Ivanhoe" were prompted by Skene's German reminiscences.

Skene says: "After having for some time dwelt on Scottish subjects in his romances, Sir Walter mentioned to me that he was contemplating an English ground for his next tale, of which he stated the proposed outline. I happened to observe that I thought a new and very interesting subject might be extracted from the barbarous treatment to which the Jewish race had been subjected in England and other Christian countries. He swung about the room in silence for a space, as was his usual habit when reflecting, and then with a slap on my shoulder, pronounced the idea not a bad one, and ' Ivanhoe ' was the result." [*]

Let us now hear what Lockhart has to say on this matter.

" The introduction of the charming Jewess and her father originated, I find, in a conversation that Scott held with his friend Skene during the severest season of his bodily sufferings in the early part of this year (1819). ' Mr Skene,' says that gentleman's wife, ' sitting by his bedside, and trying to amuse him as well as he could in the intervals of pain, happened to get on the subject of the Jews, as he had observed them when he spent some time in Germany in his youth. Their situation had naturally made a strong impression ; for in those days they retained their own dress and manners entire, and were treated with considerable austerity by their Christian neighbours, being still locked up at night in their own quarter by great gates ; and Mr Skene,

* (" Memories of Sir Walter Scott " p. 185).

partly in seriousness, but partly from the mere wish to turn his mind at the moment upon something that might occupy and divert it, suggested that a group of Jews would be an interesting feature if he could contrive to bring them into his next novel.' Upon the appearance of ' Ivanhoe,' he reminded Mr Skene of this conversation, and said, ' You will find this book owes not a little to your German reminiscences."*

* ("Life" Chap. XLVI.)

The Monastery (1820)

THE scene of "The Monastery" is laid at Melrose, near the home of Sir Walter Scott for the last years of his life. The story deals with the stirring times of the Reformation in the reign of Mary Queen of Scots, who represented the Roman Catholic party, while her half brother the Earl of Moray, afterwards Regent, represented the Protestant party.

Here again, as a distinctively Scottish story, we might hardly expect to find German influence, or that Scott should feel disposed to borrow from German authors; but we should be mistaken. Some have seen in the pathetic scene of the death of Catherine, faithful to the last to her unfaithful and cruel lover, a similar incident in "Goetz von

Berlichingen," an incident which appealed to the chivalric spirit of Sir Walter Scott, and which moved him to make use of it in "Marmion," as noted in a previous chapter.

But apart from this we have Scott's own confession that the idea of the mysterious White Lady of Avenel was borrowed from a German author, Baron de la Motte Fouqué, whom Scott greatly admired as a writer. The introduction of such a supernatural being into a story whose strength and power rest in its absolute realism and truthfulness to nature, was perhaps a mistake. It was certainly resented by many readers as "impossible" and was "far from being popular." Scott admits the borrowing, and justifies it in the following words :

"The ingenious Compte de la Motte Fouqué composed in German one of the most successful productions of his fertile brain, where a beautiful and even afflicting effect is produced by the introduction of a water-nymph, who loses the privilege of immortality, by consenting to become accessible to human feelings, and uniting her lot with that of a mortal, who treats her with ingratitude. In imitation of an example so successful, the White Lady of Avenel was introduced into the following sheets. She is represented as connected with the family of Avenel by one of those mysteries, which in ancient times, were supposed to exist, in certain circumstances, between the creatures of the elements and the children of men. Such instances of mysterious union are recognised in Ireland, in the real Milesian families, who are possessed of a Banshee; and they are known among the traditions of the Highlanders, which in many cases, attached an immortal being or spirit to the service of particular families or tribes." (Introduction to " The Monastery.")

Scott goes on to defend at greater length his White Lady from the example of Shakespeare in "Ariel," and for other reasons. Into these we need not follow him. It is enough for our purpose to point out that it was not in Ireland, or the Highlands of Scotland, or from Shakespeare, or from Gnostic philosophy but from a German author that he got his suggestion of the White Lady of Avenel. In the "Abbot," the sequel to the "Monastery," this visionary creature does not appear.

Before leaving the "Monastery," it may be worth while to refer to another German borrowing. The curious and somewhat humorous method of reminding the extravagant and ridiculous representative of Euphuism, Sir Pierce Shafton, of his humble origin, was taken, as Scott frankly confesses, from a German author.

"The contrivance of provoking the irritable vanity of Sir Piercie Shafton, by presenting him with a bodkin, indicative of his descent from a tailor, is borrowed from a

104

German romance by the celebrated Tieck, called "Das Peter Mänchen," i.e., the "Dwarf Peter." The being who gives name to the tale, is the "Burg-geist," or castle spectre, of a German family, whom he aids with his counsel, as he defends their castle by his super-natural power. But the dwarf Peter is so unfortunate an adviser, that all his counsels, though producing success in the immediate results, are in the issue attended with mishap and with guilt. The youthful baron, the owner of the haunted castle, falls in love with a maiden, the daughter of a neighbouring Count, a man of great pride, who refuses him the hand of the young lady, on account of his own superiority of descent. The lover, repulsed and affronted, returns to take counsel with the Dwarf Peter how he may silence the Count and obtain the victory in the argument, the next time they enter on the topic of pedigree. The dwarf gives his patron, or pupil, a horse-shoe, instructing him to present it to the Count when he is next giving himself superior airs on the subject of his family. It has the effect accordingly; the Count, understanding it is an allusion to a misalliance of one of his ancestors with the daughter of a blacksmith, is thrown into a dreadful passion with the young lover, the consequences of which are the seduction of the young lady, and the slaughter of her father."

The "celebrated Tieck," as Scott calls him, was a contemporary author and afterwards a great admirer of the Waverley novels, which he delighted to recommend to his countrymen. He was a prolific author —poet, novelist, historian, dramatist, translator, editor—and died in 1853.

Kenilworth (1821)

THE publication of "Kenilworth" has a special interest from the fact that it called forth the first of Scott's evasive denials of the authorship of the Waverley novels. His old friend, Mrs Hughes, made very pointed hints on the subject in a letter to Scott, who says in reply, "You mistake when you give me any credit for being concerned with these far-famed novels, but I am not the less amused with the hasty dexterity of the good folks of Cumnor and its vicinity getting all their traditionary lore into such order as to meet the taste of the public. I could have wished the author had chosen a more heroical death for his fair victim."

This is a reference to the death of Amy

Robsart by falling through a trap door left unfastened by the villains, Varney and Foster. It is dramatic enough, but not precisely "heroical."

The fascinating story with its tragic ending has been compared to Shakespeare's "Othello," to which it has some slight resemblance in the plot with Varney as the Iago. Yet it is not to "Othello" that we must look for suggestions as to the sources of "Kenilworth." Those who are acquainted with Goethe's "Egmont" cannot help being struck with the resemblance between it, in some parts, with Scott's romance. Let the reader, for example, compare Count Egmont and Clara with the Earl of Leicester and Amy Robsart ; their relationship to one another, and the fate, from the unfortunate circumstances of two innocent women, and he will see how closely Sir Walter Scott followed his German master. Each woman receives a secret visit from her lover, and the lover in each case comes disguised. The description of the interview is practically the same in both works. Thus, Egmont comes with his magnificent Spanish dress covered by a trooper's cloak. When it is thrown aside there is revealed, among other decorations, the Golden Fleece on his breast. "Ah! The Golden Fleece too!" exclaims Clara. "Did the Kaiser put this round your neck?" "Yes, child," replies Egmont, "and chain and order confer the highest privileges on him who wears them. 1 acknowledge no judge on earth over my actions except the Grand Master of the Order and the assembled chapter of Knights." (Act III.)

In "Kenilworth," Leicester in his secret visit to Amy, comes splendidly attired and is as warmly received. When his cloak dropped on the floor it revealed the various orders and distinctions which he was proud to wear. "But this other fair collar," says

Amy, "so richly wrought, with some fine jewel like a sheep hung by the middle attached to it, what does that emblem signify?"

"This collar," said the Earl, "with its double fusilles, interchanged with these knots, which are supposed to present flint-stones sparkling with fire, and sustaining the jewel you enquire about, is the badge of the noble Order of the Golden Fleece, once appertaining to the House of Burgundy. It hath high privileges, my Amy, belonging to it, this most noble Order; for even the King of Spain himself, who hath now succeeded to the honours and demesnes of Burgundy, may not sit in judgment upon a knight of the Golden Fleece, unless by assistance and consent of the Great Chapter of the Order."

Goethe was well aware of this adaptation and remarked to Eckermann, "Walter Scott used a scene from my 'Egmont' and he had a right to do so, and because he did it well he deserves praise. He has also copied the character of my 'Mignon' in one of his romances but whether with equal judgment is another question."

But it was not only to Goethe that Scott was indebted; Schiller's influence is also apparent in "Kenilworth."

Scott was of opinion that the poet Coleridge's version of "Wallenstein" was more magnificent in the English than in the German of Schiller. He delighted to quote from it, and as a writer in "Blackwood's Magazine" (Vol. XIV., 1823) remarked, the existence of "Wallenstein" had been lost sight of till it was recalled to life by being made to furnish mottos for the chapters in the Waverley Novels.

Scott showed his admiration for this German drama in his characteristic way. Chapter 18 of "Kenilworth," for example, is but a reproduction of Act IV. of "Wallenstein." The description of Leicester's astrological tower is taken straight from "Wallenstein." Both Duke Wallenstein and Lord Leicester have the same half sceptical, half superstitious belief in astrology, and do not fully trust the astrologer, although they persist in consulting him and demanding to know the omens by the reading of the stars. The astrologer in "Wallenstein," Seni, is described as "a dwarfish old man with a friendly face and snow white hair"; in "Kenilworth," Alasco, the astrologer, "was a little old man and seemed much advanced in age for his beard was long and white."

In the chapter in which Leicester causes the astrologer, Alasco, to read his future in the stars we have something analogous in the First Act of "The Death of Wallenstein." The whole of chapter 18 is indeed a very interesting commentary on similar scenes in Schiller's drama. It almost looks as if Scott wished to direct the attention of the reader to this fact when he heads the chapter with these lines from "Wallenstein." :—

> The moment comes—
> It is already come—when thou must write
> The absolute title of thy life's vast sum.
> The constellations victorious o'er thee,
> The planets shoot good fortune in fair junctions,
> And tell thee, "Now's the time."

Peveril of the Peak (1823)

IN his novels Scott struck upon a new
mine that yielded vast treasures of
wealth. At first he was almost asham-
ed to be known as a writer of fiction lest it
might injure his professional and social
position ; but before many years had passed
he made the position of the novelist one of
dignity and honour. The marvellous works
of imagination that were now flowing from
his pen, covered centuries of time and il-
lumined many countries, but especially did
they glorify his native land. The sweep
of his imagination and the range of his sympathies as shown in these books were far
beyond anything that Goethe could attain
to. Yet even in his novels, Scott did not
disdain to draw upon his early sources. In

"Peveril of the Peak," for example, one of the characters is borrowed from Goethe's unique novel of "Wilhelm Meister." It is the charming and mysterious character of Finella, whose prototype is Mignon in "Meister." Lockhart passes some severe strictures on that novel. He declares that Finella was an unfortunate conception; what is good in it is not original, and the rest, extravagantly absurd and incredible. The public did not agree with Lockhart, and Scott could write in a later edition of the novel:

"The character of Fenella, which, from its peculiarity, made a favourable impression on the public, was far from being original. The fine sketch of Mignon in Wilhelm Meister's Lehrjahre, a celebrated work from the pen of Goethe, gave the idea of such a being. But the copy will be found greatly different from my great prototype; nor can I be accused of borrowing anything save the general idea, from an author, the honour of his own country, and an example to the authors of other kingdoms, to whom all must be proud to own an obligation."

It is interesting to know what Goethe himself thought of this borrowing. He is discussing with Eckermann the principles on which an author may make adaptations of already existing characters, and says :—

"This mode of altering and improving where by continued invention the imperfect is heightened to the perfect, is the right one. But the re-making and carrying further what is already complete—as for instance, Walter Scott has done with my 'Mignon,' whom in addition to her other qualities, he makes deaf and dumb—this mode of altering I cannot commend."

It may be mentioned in passing that Scott gave the name of "Finella" to one of his favourite steeds.

Quentin Durward (1823)

THIS story has a peculiar interest for us, created by the war. It introduces us to scenes and places with which the events of 1917 have made all familiar. The very name of the hero which gives the title to the book brings before us the town of St. Quentin for which the French so vainly fought. As the hero explains, the town "takes its name from my honoured saint and patron, Saint Quentin" (here he crossed himself), "and methinks were I dwelling there, my holy patron would keep some look-out for me—he has not so many named after him as your popular saints—and yet he must have forgotten me, poor Quentin Durward, his spiritual godson."

Quite near the beginning of the story we

come to Bapaume, and Peronne, (which latter town plays an important part), and to Verdun—names of places, with those of Liège and the river Somme, which henceforth will always be associated with the great war. But here we are only concerned with tracing German influences in the novel.

The scenes are laid in France and Flanders, and the period is about 1468. The hero in the drama is the brave and noble-minded Scotsman, Quentin Durward, who had come to Tours, where his uncle was one of the Scottish body guard of Louis XI. He joins this body guard of Scottish archers and performs wonderful exploits, but it is the spirit of the French King which moves and controls the actions of all. On this powerful but unscrupulous, cruel, and blasphemous sovereign, Scott pours forth most withering contempt, both in the story itself and more strongly in the Introduction. He compares Louis to Mephistophiles, and in

117

this comparison pays an indirect compliment to his favourite German author. He says :—

"In this point of view, Goethe's conception of the character and reasoning of Mephistophiles, the tempting spirit in the singular play of 'Faust,' appears to me more happy than that which has been formed by Byron, and even than the Satan of Milton. These last great authors have given to the Evil Principle something which elevates and dignifies his wickedness; a sustained and unconquerable resistance against Omnipotence itself—a lofty scorn of suffering compared with submission, and all those points of attraction in the Author of Evil, which have induced Burns and others to consider him as the Hero of the "Paradise Lost." The great German poet has, on the contrary, rendered his seducing spirit a being who, otherwise totally impassioned, seems only to have existed for the purpose of increasing, by his persuasions and temptations, the mass of moral evil, and who calls by his seductions those slumbering passions which otherwise might have allowed the human being who was the object of the Evil Spirit's operations to pass the tenor of his life in tranquillity. For this purpose Mephistophiles is, like Louis XI., endowed with an acute and depreciating spirit of caustic wit, which is employed incessantly in undervaluing and vilifying all actions, the consequences of which do not lead certainly and directly to selfgratification."

Strassburg is introduced; it was at that period a free town, but the German character marked it strongly. The treatment of women, of which Scott gives us a glimpse, was that which prevailed in Germany in the family of Frederick the Great of Prussia, and which has made the position of women in Germany to this day lower than in any other civilized country of the world.

"I have been told by my old nurse," says the younger Countess, "that although the Rhinegrave was the best lance at the great tournament at Strassbourg, and so won the hand of my respected ancestor, yet the match was no happy one, as he used often to scold, and sometimes even to beat, my great-grandmother of blessed memory."

"And wherefore not?" said the elder Countess, "why should these victorious arms, accustomed to deal blows when abroad, be bound to restrain their energies at home? A thousand times rather would I be beaten twice a day, by a husband whose arm was as much feared by others as by me, than be the wife of a coward who dared neither to lift hand to his wife, nor to any one else!"

The whole conversation of the two ladies on this subject is as amusing as it is instructive, but our only comment is the German proverb, "Ländlich-sittlich."

A German soldier is introduced in the seventeenth chapter, one of those German adventurers who were known by the name of "lanzknechts" (spearmen) and who constituted a formidable part of the infantry of the period. He speaks a sort of German-French. The oaths and other expletives with which he garnishes his sentences are always German after the manner of Dirk Hatteraick in "Guy Mannering." We have such examples as "Donner and blitz!" "Was Honker!" "Hagel and Sturm-wetter!" "Mein Gott!" etc. He makes a compact with the Bohemian who insists on his swearing by the Three Kings of Cologne. "Du bist ein komische Mann!" says the lanzknecht, but he takes the oath.

Scott's stock of colloquial German, especially of the imprecatory kind, was probably acquired from his German secretary; he is never over-particular in his orthography.

There is an allusion to the national vices

of Scotland and Germany in Lady Hame-
line's assertion that the Scots are like the
Germans who spend all their mirth over the
Rhein-wein, and bring only their staggering
steps to a dance in the evening, and their
aching heads to the ladies' bower in the
morning. The words were addressed to
Quentin, who resented the charge as far as
he himself was concerned.

At the siege of the Castle of Liege, the
drunken rabble, it is said, engage partly for
" saus und braus." The currier's daughter,
Gertrude, is called " our Jungfrau Trud-
chen." The old currier declares that these
" schelms " and " lanzknechts " are very
devils at rummage. He quotes the proverb,
" Ein wort, ein mann," which is " our own
Low Dutch (Low German) fashion." We
have talk about " Schwarz Bier," Dorf
(village), and the " Schwarzreiters " (black
riders) described as soldiers, or rather
banditti, levied in the Lower circles of Ger-

many, who resembled the "lanzknechts" in every particular, except that the former acted as light cavalry.

"Nein, nein! das geht nicht!" says the honest Fleming in better German than Flemish.

There is an interesting reference to Ratisbon, in Bavaria. For centuries, up to long after the Reformation, there was a "Scotch College" there for the training of Scottish priests, and the Scotch Kirk (Schottenkirche), a curious Romanesque building, which dates from the 12th century, may still be seen. Sir Walter doubtless knew this Scoto-German connection, and it may have been for this reason that he introduces the once famous and still interesting city. He makes Rouge Sanglier say. "I was bred a pursuivant at the Heralds' College of Ratisbon, and received the diploma of Ehrenhold from that same learned fraternity."

"You could not derive it from a source

more worthy," answered Toison d'Or, bowing still lower than he had done before.

It is curious how Scott here, as elsewhere, introduces German words and phrases where one would think them unnecessary, or even out of place. Thus he speaks of the "Lusthaus " of some wealthy citizen of Liège, and makes Louis Duke of Orleans order the Countess Isobelle to the " Zuchthaus," or penitentiary.

" Quentin Durward " had an extraordinary popularity on the Continent from the first. Lockhart says the sensation it created in Paris was similar to that which attended the original "Waverley " in Edinburgh, and "Ivanhoe" in London. "Germany," adds Lockhart, " had been fully awake to his merits years before, but the public there also felt their sympathies appealed to with hitherto unmatched strength and effect."

It is not surprising that Scott should contemplate a novel dealing with some period of German history. "I can't but think," he said to his friend, Willie Laidlaw, "that I could make better play still with something German." Laidlaw protested, like a true Scotchman, "Na, na, sir,—take my word for it, you are always best, like Helen Macgregor, when your foot is on your native heath."

Scott was diverted from his purpose for the time, but it was never abandoned and was actually carried out in "Anne of Geierstein," although that novel was not so entirely German as it might have been if Scott had begun it then instead of six years later.

St Ronan's Well (1823)

"ST. Ronan's Well," published in 1823, was carefully revised some months before the author's death, and an introduction added. As he says in the introduction, he follows a plan different from any other in his previous novels. It was the description of a Scottish watering place, believed to be Innerleithen, and the characters to be met with there. Among the miscellaneous crowd of guests, Scott does not introduce a single German, but oddly enough, when two Englishmen met for the first time, Captain Jekyl and the much-travelled Touchwood, after talking for a little while in English, they dropped into German,—for what reason is not very evident. The Captain lighting a cigar says :—''Vergeben sie, mein herr—ich ben erzogen in kaiserlichen dienst—muss rauchen ein kleine wenig."

Touchwood immediately replies :—

" Rauchen sie immer fort, habe auch mein pfeifchen—Sehen sie den lieben topf!"

The German is peculiar, as the reader will observe. Scott furnishes a translation in a footnote, which we may add :

"Forgive me, sir, I was bred in the Imperial service, and must smoke a little."

"Smoke as much as you please ; I have got my pipe, too! Soo what a beautiful head!"

In this novel, as in Quentin Durward and in others, Scott introduces German names for English articles, a habit which he had perhaps acquired while talking with Weber.

The Betrothed (1825)

IN "The Betrothed," we find further evidence of Scott's familiarity with German lore and literature. That novel is founded on a legend that was told in many parts of Europe. Although Scott says he makes chief use of the tale principally from the edition preserved in the mansion house of Haighhall, now possessed by the Earls of Balcarres, he gives a spirited verse translation of the German legend. He says that he found it in a collection of German popular songs entitled "Sammlung Deutschen Volkslieder" Berlin, 1807. The ballad, he explains, is supposed to be extracted from a manuscript chronicle of Nicolas Thomann, chaplain to St. Leonard in Weissenhorn, and dated 1533. It was popular in Germany and is believed from the language to have been composed in the fifteenth century. Scott relates the story according to this version, and translates a large part of it in ballad verse. This is a worthier tale than the Scotch one, and has a more beautiful ending.

Scott adds that there is also in the rich field of German romance another edition of this story, which has been converted by Tieck into the subject of one of his romantic dramas. The reader of "The Betrothed" will readily see, that, while Scott has not made any literal borrowings from the German version, he has not been uninfluenced by it. The story has certainly not lost anything from his spirited rendering of it, and indeed shows Scott at his best as a translator of German ballads, with which kind of work he first tried his "'prentice hand."

The Talisman (1825)

THE Talisman is a stirring story of the Crusaders in Palestine. The heroic figure of Richard Coeur de Lion stands forth prominently, and many exciting events take place in which he is directly or indirectly concerned. It will be remembered that Richard on his way home was ship-wrecked and for a long time was imprisoned in Austria. On his arrival in England (1194) he was re-crowned at Winchester to cancel the homage he had rendered to the German Emperor for England, as a condition for gaining his liberty. It was Austria, however, that took a leading part with England in the Crusades, and the Duke of Austria plays a leading part in the development of the story. Here Scott gets his opportunity of making use of his knowledge of Germany, and German customs. The Duke of Austria considered himself ungratefully treated because the "minne singers" ("the German minstrels were so called," Scott reminds us) were filled with praises of King Richard.

Scott refers to a characteristic of the Germans which he notices in other works. "The Germans," he says, "though still possessing the martial and frank character of their ancestors—who subdued the Roman Empire—had retained withal no slight tinge of their barbarism. The practices and principles of chivalry were not carried to such a nice pitch amongst them as amongst the French and English knights, nor were they strict observers of the prescribed rules of society, which amongst those nations were supposed to express the height of civilization."

With how much greater truth could this be said now?

Our author makes Richard, as a Norman prince—" a people with whom temperance was habitual "—despise the German's love for the pleasures of the table, and particularly his liberal indulgence in the use of wine. On another occasion he makes Richard say that " the German boar breakfasts ere he hears mass," and he describes his behaviour at a royal banquet thus : " Sitting at the table of the Archduke, Conrade was at once stunned and amused with the clang of Teutonic sounds assaulting his ears on all sides notwithstanding the solemnity of a princely banquet—in the midst of a clamour and confusion which would better have become a German tavern during a fair than the tent of a sovereign prince."

That also remains typical of German social gatherings even in the highest circles!

Behind the Duke's right shoulder stood his "Spruchsprecher," that is, his man of conversation, or "sayer of sayings," who was by turns a flatterer, a poet and an orator; and those who desired to be popular with the Duke generally studied to gain the goodwill of the "spruchsprecher."

Lest too much of this officer's wisdom should become tiresome, the Duke's other shoulder was occupied by his "Hofnarr," or court jester, called Jonas Schwanker. The "Hofnarr" as well as the "Spruchsprecher" was as much an institution as the minne-singers. One of the latter sings in "High German," a song of which two verses are given in translation, followed by the acclamation "Hoch lebe der Herzog Leopold!"

We have not been able to trace this song; but there probably exists no translation except that from Scott's own pen as in the case of his chapter headings ascribed to "Old Play."

In "The Talisman," as in other novels when Scott finds himself in a German atmosphere, he uses German words for local colouring, and sometimes when they seem unnecessary. He has used here such German words as "Rauch" for smoke, "Maul" for mouth (vulgar) "widersins," that is, as Scott explains, from left to right, and so on.

Anne of Geierstein (1829)

WHEN his hand had become feebler and his imagination less strong, Scott went back to his early sources of inspiration. In this, one of his last novels, " Anne of Geierstein," we are introduced to the Germany of the Middle Ages. In a long introduction, written the year before his death, Scott admitted that it was Goethe that he followed rather than historical authorities. Even in the course of the story, he could not help referring to the master whom he held in such respect. When describing (chap. 17) the old castles of the Rhine as real and apparently impregnable strongholds of that robber chivalry, he recalls the legends that gathered round them of which " since Goethe, an author born to arouse the slumbering fame of his country, has dramatised the story of Goétz of Berlichingen, we have had so many spirit-stirring tales."

Scott had drunk so deeply of German romance, and was so familiar with German history as reflected in his favourite author, that the reader feels himself transported to the Germany of those times which in many respects has, in its essential spirit, not altered to this day. The formality and pomp with which German princelings sought to impress their subjects, still persists; and those of other countries who have had to endure it can sympathise with Arnold Biedermann when he says, that what to his brother seemed the consummation of earthly splendour, was to him a weary display of tiresome and useless ceremonials. Throughout the story there leap forth many touches and incidents revealing Scott's familiarity with German customs. For example, it is said of Hermann von Arnheim, the maternal grandfather of Anne, that " he was buried with his helmet, sword and shield, as is the German custom with the last male of a noble family."

Scott draws a striking contrast between the social spirit peculiar to the French nation and the saturnine and sullen reception which strangers were apt to meet with at a German caravanserai. In comparison with French customs, the habits of the Germans were often coarse and even disgusting. The food both in kind and manner of serving it, was coarse and indifferent, except in the article of wine, and very different from the way in which even the plainest dishes are presented in a French inn. How Philipson fared at a gasthaus under the proverbial rudeness of a German innkeeper could be matched in some parts of Germany at the present day, in the rural districts at all events, but could nowhere be equalled in any part of France. Goethe's question still remains unanswered, "When will it be said of us Germans, 'It is a long time since they were barbarians'?"

The German sometimes prides himself on his rudeness, which he calls honesty. The speech made by mine host, John Mengs, to the Englishman Philipson would be defended in this twentieth century. "You might as well expect to see one of our bears come aloft and do tricks like a jackanapes, as one of us stubborn old Germans play the feats of a French or Italian host. Yet I pray you to note, that if our behaviour is rude our charges are honest, and our articles what they profess to be. We do not expect to make Moselle to pass for Rhenish, by dint of a bow and a grin, nor will we sauce your mess with poison, like the wily Italian, and call you all the time Illustrissimo and Magnifico."

The whole chapter is in Scott's best style

in description and portraiture. Although the scenes of the story are laid in various countries, sometimes in Switzerland, or Burgundy, or Alsace, and various parts of Germany, it is the German spirit and character that predominate, because it was these that Scott knew best. We are constantly reminded of this by the author, who cannot refrain from frequently introducing German words, probably to give an air of greater reality, where English words might suffice. He takes special pleasure in translating or giving the literal meaning of such words, even when they are proper names, as "Dopellgänger," "Biedermann," etc. He heads one of his chapters (18) with a verse translated from a German ballad, and informs the reader in a footnote that this is one of the best and most popular of the German ditties, quoting two lines of the original text.

It is the voice of a true German also, not

of a Swiss, which we hear in those words which might be a passage from Bernhardi's book, on the greatness of war.

"It was by war, noble war, that our fathers came forth from the house of their captivity; it was by war, successful and glorious war, that a race who had been held scarce so much worth thinking on as the oxen which they goaded, emerged at once into liberty and consequence, and were honoured because they were feared, as much as they had been formerly despised because they were unresisting."

How modern this sounds! and how easily we can appreciate the difficulty of young Philipson, the Englishman, in understanding or approving of Donnerhugel who is making professions of peace while all the time he is secretly blowing the coals of war!

It is curious to observe how Scott's imagination was mastered by the memory of a character which he had originally borrowed from Goethe, and had introduced into "Peveril of the Peak." The little Persian damsel with her fairy form and fantastic appearance, and remarkable gift for dancing, Sybella of Winheim, is but a re-production of Finella, whose prototype is found in "Mignon." We have referred more fully to this character when dealing with "Peveril of the Peak."

The influence of Schiller's "Wilhelm Tell" is apparent in some of the Swiss scenes. Especially do we mark this in Chapter 10, where there is a direct reference to the well-known meeting at midnight and the solemn exchanges of oaths by the conspirators. They swore to each other under the blue firmament of heaven that they would restore the liberty of their oppressed country. The description of Arnold Biedermann, the leader, may be taken as a portrait of the honest Stauffacher in "Wilhelm Tell."

Chapter 20 is one of the most powerful in

141

this novel. The author describes in simple but graphic language the proceedings of the secret tribunal, or "Vehmegericht." The subject had first been brought under his notice through the genius of Goethe, quite early in Scott's literary career, and it seems to have exercised such a fascination that he returns to it near the close of his life.

This tribunal whose seat was confined to Westphalia, but whose arm extended far and wide and struck terror where its power reached, was a thoroughly organised institution. It has been compared to the Reign of Terror in France, and to the Spanish Inquisition, but the reign of terror was short lived, and the Inquisition was a method for searching out heretics with a view to bringing them to repentance, or punishing them in proportion to their offences. The strength of the "Vehmegericht" lay in its absolute secrecy, and the spirit of terrorism which it created. No one knew who formed

Goethe's House in Weimar.

the tribunal, or how its mysterious meetings were conducted. No one was safe against its power; anyone might be suddenly carried before the court which always met at midnight. The laws of the "Vehmegericht" bore no penalty save that of death, but there was no publication of the sentence. The person was mysteriously apprehended and simply disappeared from society never more to be heard of.

Scott took great pains to obtain accurate information about the "Vehmegericht" and wrote to his friend Skene (26th Dec., 1828) on the subject: "If you can easily bring with you the striking description of the subterranean vaults at Baden (I think supposed to be the place of meeting of the secret tribunal) with your plan and drawings, they will do me yeoman's service in something I am now about." This "something" refers to "Anne of Geierstein"; and Skene explains that Scott wished to see the paper he

143

had contributed to the Society of Antiquaries on the subject of the secret tribunals of Germany, and upon which accordingly he grounded the scene of his novel.

Skene goes on to make a remarkable statement with regard to Scott's " Anne of Geierstein." " Upon his describing to me the scheme which he had formed for that work, I suggested to him that he might with advantage connect the history of René, King of Provence, which would lead to many interesting topographical details, which my residence in that country would enable me to supply, besides giving him the opportunity of illustrating so eccentric a character as ' le bon Roi René,' full of traits which were admirably suited to Sir Walter's graphic style of illustration, and that he could besides introduce the amusing ceremonies of the Fête Dieu with great advantage, as I had fortunately seen its revival the first time it was celebrated after the

144

interruption of the Revolution. He liked
the idea much, and accordingly a journal
which I had written during my residence in
Provence, with a volume of accompanying
drawings and Papon's "History of Provence," were forthwith sent for, and in the
course of a few days I received a most
amusing note from him, announcing "the
suppression of the already printed volume
of ' Anne of Geierstein ' and the readjust-
ment of the tale." He proposed to retain
Papon's "History" and my manuscript
volumes till the novel was finished, as he
meant to locate his "dramatis personae"
in many of the positions I had described,
even in the secret chambers of the Geheim
Gericht, so that on perusal I should find the
new Anne an old acquaintance. I never
met with a stronger instance of the uncommon versatility of Sir Walter's genius than
he displayed in the facility with which he
took up the spirit of a narrative altogether

new to him and the characteristics of a country which he had never seen." (Memories of Sir Walter Scott, pp. 155-6.)

It will be seen from this that on account of the information he received from Skene, Scott suppressed the already printed volume of " Anne of Geierstein " and readjusted the tale. This is very remarkable, and is nowhere mentioned by Scott himself, nor does Lockhart refer to the matter. When Scott issued a new edition of " Anne of Geierstein " in 1831, with its long Introduction, he does not even mention Skene's name, although he refers to others to whom he was indebted. He pays a high tribute to Mr Francis Palgrave, afterwards Sir Francis Palgrave, for the light he throws upon the Vehme Gericht. " With regard to a general subject of great curiosity and interest," he says, " in the eyes at least of all antiquarian students, upon which I have touched at some length in this narrative, I mean

146

the "Vehmic" tribunals of Westphalia, a name so awful in men's ears during many centuries, and which, through the genius of Goethe, has again been revived in public fancy with a full share of its ancient terrors, I am bound to state my opinion that a wholly new and most important light has been thrown upon this matter, since "Anne of Geierstein" first appeared, by the elaborate researches of my ingenious friend, Mr Francis Palgrave, whose proof sheets, containing the passages I allude to, have been kindly forwarded to me, and whose complete work will be before the public ere this Introduction can pass through the press."

He then quotes about a dozen pages from Palgrave's work, printing the more important passages in italics, as to Palgrave's theory about the origin of the Vehme Gericht (with which origin we have here nothing to do), Scott says :—it seems to him "to have every appearance of truth and justice; and if such should, on maturer investigation, turn out to be the fact, it will certainly confer no small honour on an English scholar to have discovered the key to a mystery which had long exercised in vain the laborious and profound students of German antiquity."

Scott was always ready to express his obligations to those who helped him in any way, and was not the man to slight any one, least of all "good Samaritan Skene," to whom he first turned for comfort when staggering under the blow of financial ruin. It may be that Skene, writing down his recollections of his friend long years after, had deceived himself, and overestimated the assistance he gave to Scott.

It may be added that in the "Archaeologia Scotica," 1823, vol. III., there appears an account by Skene of a "suite of apartments excavated from the rocks on which the Castle of Baden, in Swabia, stands, supposed to have been connected with the jurisdiction of the Secret Tribunal in that country."

To the Introduction, and to the romance itself, especially chapter 20, the reader is referred. All that we aim at doing here is to point it out as a striking example of German influence on Sir Walter's Scott's work.

"Anne of Geierstein" is a novel that might be read with profit at this time. It has never been so popular with English readers as some of Scott's other novels, and Lockhart seems to apologise for it to some extent; but it is a great work. It may be objected that the heroine, who also gives the title to the book, plays a very unimportant part, and is sometimes lost sight of altogether for a time, but the spirit of the heroine dominates the story, and the reader's interest is never allowed to abate. "Anne of Geierstein" is not so much a

149

narrative as a series of grand episodes covering a vast field of time and space. It contains some of Scott's finest writing, and many of the chapters show his genius at its highest.

My Aunt Margaret's Mirror (1827)

THIS is one of the short stories which Scott contributed to a miscellany of prose and verse, a species of publication which had come to be generally known by the title of "Annual." It was issued about Christmas, and Scott says it had flourished for a long while in Germany before it was imitated in this country by an enterprising bookseller, a German by birth, Mr Ackermann. The fact that it had a German origin may have helped to evoke Scott's sympathy for one of its rivals, "The Keepsake," to which he contributed the above story which, however, has no German colouring. It was in this annual that he published a long neglected performance of his youthful days "The House of Aspen," which he had adapted from the German, and which has been referred to elsewhere.

Scott's Novels in Germany:
Goethe's Opinion of Them.

SCOTT'S novels very early found their way into Germany and were eagerly read by many. Some poor attempts were made to imitate them. In the case of one of these imitations, "Walladmor," professing to be a translation from the English (Berlin 1824) the author actually put the name of Sir Walter Scott on the title page to procure for it, probably, greater authority. Lockhart's conjecture was that some sheets of a novel that Scott had begun but cancelled on the remonstrance of James Ballantyne, had found their way into Germany. Sir Walter was indignant when he heard of the publication of the worthless book thus attributed to him. He took up his own discarded novel again and completed it as " The Betrothed." The publication of this pseudo Scott romance is remarkable in another way, for, although Scott had long been suspected in this country as the author of the Waverley novels, it was not till the memorable 23rd February, 1827, that he publicly made the avowal that he was " the total and undivided author."

Still more striking, and illustrating at the same time the celebrity which Scott had gained in Germany, is the fact that the year that " Walladmor " appeared in Berlin there were published " The Fortunes of Nigel " and " Peveril of the Peak" in the German language and in German type, in Reutlingen, a small town in the south, in Würtemburg, assigning the authorship to Sir Walter Scott.

Here again we have the authorship of the novels publicly proclaimed in Germany nearly three years earlier than it was declared in this country.

It may be interesting to add that copies of these two novels were recently presented to the Edinburgh Corporation Museum by Mr J. M. Mitchell, a well known citizen, and may be seen by any one curious in the matter.

I have also before me now some of Scott's novels published in 1823 and 1824 in Zwickau, an old manufacturing town in Saxony, the birthplace of Schumann, the composer. These volumes belong to a series bearing the title, "Pocket Library of English Classics." They are well printed and neatly bound. The title of "Kenilworth" may be given in full : " 'Kenilworth,' a Romance, by the authòr of 'Waverley,' 'Ivanhoe,' etc., 1824. 'No scandal about Elizabeth, I hope,' — *Critic.* In four volumes. Zwickau : Printed for Brothers Schu-

mann." The name of this division of the
Pocket Library is "The Works of Walter
Scott, Esq." The frontispiece to "Kenilworth " is a portrait of Queen Elizabeth,
"Königin von England." The other
volumes are similar in style, but " Ivanhoe " (also in four volumes) has the date of
1823.

A publishing house in Dresden also published in 1823 " The Bride of Lammer-
moor," " Waverley " (under the title of
" Eduard ") and " The Heart of Mid-
lothian," " aus dem Englischen von
Walther Scott."

As further illustrating the extraordinary
vogue of Sir Walter Scott in Germany
about this period, I reproduce the title
page of a work of unique character, published in Königsberg, " the City of Pure
Reason," as Germans call the city of
Immanuel Kant. The philosopher, by the
way, was of Scottish extraction, and there

was quite a colony of Scottish settlers then in the north east of Prussia. The title of this work is in duplicate, English and German facing each other " Pocket Dictionary of the Scottish Idiom in which the significance of the words is given in English and German, chiefly calculated to promote the understanding of the works of Sir Walter Scott, Robert Burns, Allan Ramsay, etc., with an Appendix containing notes explicative of Scottish customs, manners, traditions, etc., by Robert Motherby. Königsberg, 1826. Printed for Brothers Borntraeger." The Dictionary is followed by " Notes " in English and German ending on page 232. Four pages of errata in English with four in German end the book.

I wonder if Scott knew of this early homage paid to his genius by Germany? I cannot trace any evidence of the fact in English sources.

Heinrich Heine, the great lyric poet of
Germany, had also a strong appreciation
of Sir Walter Scott's romances, and it was
undoubtedly under the influence, more or
less direct, of Scott during the foreign
wave of romantic sentiment that he wrote
his tragedies "Almonsor," and "Rat-
cliffe." He did not forget his debt to
Scott, and while most unsparing in his
satires on contemporary writers, including
Goethe, he never levelled any of his shafts
against the great Scottish poet-novelist,
although he alluded to Scott's "Life of
Napoleon" with more pity than scorn, as
"a blasphemy in twelve volumes."
Heine's admiration for Napoleon was as
extreme as Scott's hatred. In "Norder-
ney" occur the fine sayings concerning Sir
Walter Scott—particularly that of the more
or less unconscious pathos, "the dominant
note in his romances—the note that has
sent a thrill of pain through the world."

It is to Heine that we owe one of the most delightful descriptions of the popularity of Sir Walter Scott in Germany, which must be quoted here. It appears in one of the "Letters from Berlin," which were written and published in 1822 in a Berlin newspaper, and later in separate form with additions.

"But how am I to pass from the Ee-aw of long ears," he says, "from the Baa of the thick wool-pates, to the works of Sir Walter Scott? For of these I must now speak, because all Berlin speaks of them, because they are the *Jungfernkranz* of the reading world. They are everywhere read, admired, criticised, cut up, and again re-read. From the countess to the milliner, from the count to the messenger, everyone reads the romances of the great Scott; and in particular, our sentimental ladies. These lie down with 'Waverley,' and get up with 'Red Gauntlet,' and during the whole day they have the 'Dwarf' between their fingers. The romance, 'Kenilworth' has caused an especial furore ; as there are few persons here who are blessed with a knowledge of English, the great majority of our reading world help themselves with French and German translations. Of these there is no lack. Of the latest of Walter Scott's novels, 'The Pirate,' four translations were announced at the same time. Two were published here, that of Frau von Montenglant by Schlesinger, and that of Doctor Spieker by Drucker and Humboldt. The third translation is by Litz in Hamburg, and the fourth will be brought out in the pocket editions of the Brothers Schumann in Zwickau. In such circumstances it is obvious that certain collisions are unavoidable. Frau von Hohenhausen is at work now upon a translation of 'Ivanhoe,' and from this excellent translator of Byron we may anticipate an equally excellent translation of Scott. I even believe that this latter will, if anything, be superior; for the gentle soul of this beautiful woman, so deeply in sympathy with the purely ideal, will reflect the serene, pious, chaste types of the friendly Scott with greater clearness than the dusky, infernal figures of the morose, heart-sick Englishman. The beautiful tender Rebecca could not fall into more beautiful or tender hands, and the sensitive poet need in this instance only translate straight from her heart.

"The name of Walter Scott has recently been fêted in a most remarkable way. On the occasion of a festival there was a brilliant masquerade, wherein most of the heroes of Scott's novels were personated in their characteristic costumes. This fête and these figures were talked about during eight successive days. A

special point of interest was that the son of
Sir Walter Scott, who happened to be in
Berlin at the moment, paraded at the brilliant fête as a Scottish Highlander, with
the naked legs required in this costume,
that is, wearing no trousers, but only a
sort of apron which reached to the middle
of the thighs. This young man, an officer
in the English Hussars, has been made
much of here, and enjoys his reflected
glory. Where are the sons of Schiller?
Where are the sons of our great poets,
who, if not without trousers, yet in all
likelihood wander about without shirts?
Where are our greater poets themselves?
Hush, hush, that's not to be talked
about ! "

Referring to Scott's visit to Paris after
Waterloo in 1815 with his friend, John
Scott of Gala, Lockhart says, " It will
seem less surprising that Scott should
have been honoured with much attention

by the leading soldiers and statesmen of Germany then in Paris. The fame of his poetry had already been established for some years in that country. . . . As yet, the literary reputation of Scott had made but little way among the French nation, but some few of their eminent men vied even with the enthusiastic Germans in their courteous and unwearied attentions to him."

Scott's genius reached its fullest development in the wonderful series of novels which called forth the unbounded praise of Goethe, his first master in literature. Tieck boasted that he had introduced the first copy of Waverley into Germany in 1818. It is certain that Goethe was a diligent reader of the Waverley novels, and he has left on record some interesting criticisms of them. Speaking of the ''Fair Maid of Perth,'' he says :—''Walter Scott's 'Fair Maid of Perth,' is excellent, is it not? There is finish! there is a hand! What a firm foundation for the whole, and in particulars not a touch which does not lead to the catastrophe! Then what details of dialogue and description, both of which are excellent."

But it is for Waverley that the highest praise is reserved. "When you have finished the 'Fair Maid of Perth,' said Goethe to Eckermann, "you must at once read Waverley, which is indeed from quite a different point of view, but which may, without hesitation, be set beside the best works that have ever been written in the world."

Of the novels of Scott Goethe never tired ; and at the close of a long life we find him returning to them with renewed pleasure. "We read far too many poor things," he said, "thus losing time and gaining nothing. We should only read what we admire, as I did in my youth,

163

and as I now experience with Walter
Scott. I have just begun 'Rob Roy,'
and will read his best novels in succession.
All is great-material, import, characters,
execution ; and then what infinite diligence
in the preparatory studies! what truth of
detail in the execution. We see, too,
what English history is ; and what a thing
it is when such an inheritance falls to the
lot of a clever poet."

Lockhart quotes from "The Winter
Studies and Rambles" (1838) by Mrs
Jameson, a statement bearing out Goethe's
openly expressed admiration for Scott's
works :—"Everywhere Goethe speaks of
Sir Walter Scott with the utmost enthusiasm of admiration, as the greatest writer
of his time ; he speaks of him as being
without his like, as without his equal. I
remember Goethe's daughter-in-law saying
to me playfully—'When my father got
hold of one of Scott's romances, there was

no speaking to him till he had finished the third volume ; he was worse than any girl at a boarding-school with her first novel!' "

It was no blind homage that Goethe paid to Scott. Goethe was a keen and discriminating critic, delighting to recognise a soul of goodness wherever it was to be found, and he could not praise where praise was not fully due. Thus he was alive to the defects as well as to the excellencies of Scott's novels, and he illustrates how Scott's great talent for representing details often leads him into faults. But Goethe found no pleasure in destructive criticism ; his judgments always leaned to the side of a broad and tolerant charity. He possessed a great heart, and was essentially quick to recognise greatness in others, and to express his admiration for it freely and fully. At a period when national feeling ran high, Goethe rose above the prejudices

165

of his nation, and at the risk of being called unpatriotic he welcomed genius, whether it came from France or Scotland, or was found among his own countrymen.

It was natural that Goethe should desire a closer acquaintance with an author whom he held in such high esteem. When sending a parcel to Carlyle, he enclosed six medals, three struck at Weimar and three at Geneva; two of the medals he wished to be presented to Sir Walter Scott with his "Verbindlichsten Grüssen." Scott was at the time in London, and Carlyle sent the gifts by Jeffrey "our grand British Critic," to whom Sir Walter expressed himself properly sensible of such an honour "from one of his Masters in Arts." Somehow Scott did not acknowledge them to Carlyle, and the latter was rather offended. We find Scott, however, writing a long letter to Goethe, of date 9th July, 1827, in reply to Goethe, in which he gives a number of interesting particulars about himself and his household. Goethe was highly delighted with the letter, which he looked upon as a sign of brotherly confidence, but he was disappointed that Scott made no mention of Carlyle. "He must certainly be known to him," he says to Eckermann. Scott accompanied his letter with a copy of his "Life of Napoleon Buonaparte," which Goethe had been so eager to possess. He read the work with interest but not with sympathy, for he could not share Scott's intense hatred of Napoleon and the French. The book recalled many incidents in Goethe's own life. As he said, it had become a golden net with which he was busily hauling up, in an abundant draught, out of the swelling waters of Lethe, shadowy images of his past life. He and Eckermann had been talking of the work one evening, when Goethe said:

" It is true that the author may be re-proached with great inaccuracy and equally great partiality ; but even these two defects give to his work peculiar value in my eyes. The success of the book in England was great beyond all expectation ; and hence we see that Walter Scott, in this very hatred for Napoleon and the French, has been the true inter-preter and representative of the English popular opinion and national feeling. His book will not be by any means a document for the history of France, but it will be one for the history of England. At all events, it is a voice which could not be wanting in this important historical pro-cess. ("Gespräche mit Goethe 1830.")

Goethe wrote further in " Kunst und Altertum," (the magazine which he edited): " Walter Scott spent his childhood among the stirring scenes of the American War, and was a youth of seventeen or eighteen when the French Revolution broke out. Now well advanced in the fifties, having all along been favourably placed for observation, he proposes to lay before us his views and recollections of the important events through which he has lived. The richest, the easiest, the most celebrated narrator of the country, undertakes to write the history of his own time."

" What expectations the announcement of such a work must have excited in me, will be understood by any one who remembers that I, twenty years older than Scott, conversed with Paoli in the twentieth year of my age, and with Napoleon himself in the sixtieth."

" Through that long series of years, coming more or less into contact with the great doings of the world, I failed not to think seriously on what was passing around me, and, after my own fashion, to connect so many extraordinary mutations into something like arrangement and inter-dependence.

"What could now be more delightful to me than leisurely and calmly to sit down and listen to the discourse of such a man, while clearly, truly, and with all the skill of a great artist, he recalls to me the incidents on which through life I have meditated, and the influence of which is still daily in operation?"

In an interesting letter to Carlyle about the same time Goethe emphasises the value of the book and his appreciation of the writer.

"If you see Sir Walter Scott," writes Goethe, "pray offer him my warmest thanks for his valued and pleasant letter, written frankly in the beautiful conviction that man must be precious to man. I have also received his "Life of Napoleon"; and during these winter evenings and nights, I have read it through attentively from beginning to end. It was extremely significant to me to see the first narrator of the century taking upon himself so unusual a task, and bringing before us in quiet succession the momentous events which we ourselves had been compelled to witness. The division into chapters of large homogenous masses makes the intricate course of affairs perfectly intelligible, and the exposition of single incidents, of inestimable clearness and distinctness. I read it in the original, and thus it produced its natural effect. It is a patriotic Briton who speaks, who cannot well view the acts of the enemy with favourable eyes ; who, as an upright citizen, desires that even in political enterprises the demands of morality should be satisfied, who threatens his adversary in his audacious career of good-luck with fatal consequences, and who even in his most bitter downfall can scarcely pity him.

" The Work was further of significance to me, since, partly by recalling my own past experiences, partly by bringing anew before me many things I had overlooked, it placed me on an unexpected standpoint, led me to consider what I had taken as settled, and especially, also, enabled me to be just to the opponents, who cannot be wanting to so weighty a work, and to estimate aright the objections which from their side they may bring against it. This you see at the end of the year no more precious gift could have reached me."

Posterity has justified the judgment of Goethe regarding this work of Scott's. It is to it that we owe the interchange of letters between the two great writers. The letters, interesting in themselves, are characteristic of the two men, and may be fitly introduced here.

Scott's Correspondence with Goethe.

The following is Goethe's letter to his Scottish contemporary as translated by Lockhart :—

" To Sir Walter Scott, Bart., Edinburgh.
Weimar, January 12th, 1827.

Mr H......, well known to me as a collector of objects of art, has given me a likeness, I hope, authentic and accurate, of the late Lord Byron, and awakens anew the sorrow which I could not but feel for the loss of one whom all the world prized, and I in particular ; since how could I fail to be delighted with the many expressions of partiality for me which his writings contain !

Meantime the best consolation for us, the survivors, is to look around us, and consider, that as the departed is not alone, but has joined the noble-spiritual company of high-hearted men, capable of love, friendship, and confidence, that had left this sphere before him, so we have still kindred spirits on earth, with whom, though not visible any more than the blessed shades of past ages, we have a right to feel a brother-like connection — which is, indeed, our richest inheritance.

And so, as Mr H—— informs me he expects to be soon in Edinburgh, I thus acquit myself, mine honoured Sir, of a duty which I had long felt incumbent on me—to acknowledge the lively interest I have during many years taken in your wonderful pictures of human life. I have not wanted external stimulants enough to keep my attention awake on this subject, since not only have translations abounded in the German, but the works are largely read here in the original, and valued according as different men are capable of comprehending their spirit and genius.

Can I remember that such a man in his youth made himself acquainted with my writings, and even (unless I have been misinformed) introduced them in part to the knowledge of his own nation, and yet defer any longer, at my now very advanced years, to express my sense of such an honour? It becomes one, on the contrary, not to lose the opportunity now offered of praying for a continuance of your kindly regard, and telling you how much a direct assurance of good-will from your own hand would gratify my old age.

With high and grateful respect,

I salute you,

J. W. v. Goethe."

175

It was natural that this letter should give pleasure to Sir Walter Scott. His reply was equally gratifying to the German poet, who in a letter to Carlyle with whom he was in constant correspondence, spoke of it as " cheering and warm-hearted." The following is Scott's reply :

" To the Baron von Goethe, etc., etc., Weimar.

Venerable and much-respected Sir, — I received your highly-valued token of esteem by Mr H — —, and have been rarely so much gratified as by finding that any of my productions have been fortunate enough to attract the attention of Baron von Goethe, of whom I have been an admirer ever since the year 1798, when I became a little acquainted with the German language ; and soon after gave an example at once of my good taste and consummate assurance, by an attempt to translate Goetz von Berlichingen—entirely forgetting that it is necessary not only to be delighted with a work of genius, but to be well acquainted with the language in which it is written, before we attempt to communicate its beauty to others. I still set a value on my early translation, however, because it serves to show that I knew at least how to select an object worthy of admiration, although from the terrible blunders into which I fell, from imperfect acquaintance with the language, it was plain I had not adopted the best way of expressing my admiration.

I have heard of you often from my son-in-law, Lockhart—I do not believe you have a more devout admirer than this young connexion of mine. My friend, Sir John Hope of Pinkie, has had more lately the honour of seeing you ; and I hoped to have written to you—indeed, did use that freedom—by two of his own kinsmen who

were to travel in Germany, but illness
intervened and prevented their journey,
and my letter was returned after it was
two or three months old ;—so that I had
presumed to claim the acquaintance of
Baron von Goethe even before the flattering notice which he has been pleased to
bestow on me. It gives to all admirers
of genius and literature, delight to know
that one of the greatest European models
enjoys a happy and dignified retirement
during an age which is so universally
honoured and respected. Fate destined
a premature close to that of poor Lord
Byron, who was cut off when his life was
in the flower, and when so much was hoped
and expected from him. He esteemed
himself, as I have reason to know, happy
in the honour which you did him, and not
unconscious of the obligations which he
owed to one to whom all the authors of
his generation have been so much obliged,

that they are bound to look up to him with filial reverence.

I have given another instance that, like other barristers, I am not encumbered with too much modesty, since I have entreated Messrs Treuttel and Würtz to find some means of conveying to you a hasty, and of course, rather tedious attempt to give an account of that remarkable person Napoleon, who had for so many years such a terrible influence in the world. I do not know but what I owe him some obligations, since he put me in arms for twelve years, during which I served in one of our corps of Yeomanry, and notwithstanding an early lameness, became a good horseman, a hunter, and a shooter. Of late these faculties have failed me, as the rheumatism, that sad torment of our northern climate, has had its influence on my bones. But I cannot complain, since I see my sons pursuing the sport I have given up. My eldest son has a troop of Hussars, which is high in our army for a young man of twenty-five ; my youngest son has just been made Bachelor of Arts at Oxford, and is returned to spend some months with me before going out into the world. God having been pleased to deprive me of their mother, my youngest daughter keeps my household in order, my eldest being married, and having a family of her own. Such are the domestic circumstances of the person you so kindly inquired after ; for the rest, I have enough to live on in the way I like, notwithstanding some very heavy losses ; and I have a stately antique château (modern antique) to which any friend of Baron von Goethe will be at all times most welcome—with an entrance hall filled with armour, which might have become Jaxthausen itself, and a gigantic blood-hound to guard the entrance.

I have forgot, however, one who did not use to be forgotten when he was alive : — I hope you will forgive the faults of the composition, in consideration of the author's wish to be as candid toward the memory of this extraordinary man as his own prejudice would permit. As this opportunity of addressing you opens suddenly by a chance traveller, and must be instantly embraced, I have not time to say more than to wish Baron von Goethe a continuance of health and tranquillity, and to subscribe myself, with sincerity and profound respect, his much honoured and obliged humble servant.

WALTER SCOTT.

Mrs Jameson says, — "All Goethe's family recollect the exceeding pleasure which Sir Walter's letter gave him."

It will be seen that Sir John Hope, of Pinkie, Scott's relative, was one of the

Scottish pilgrims to Weimar. He was the bearer of welcome news of Sir Walter Scott and other friends in distant Scotland.

Goethe was also much interested in Lockhart, Scott's son-in-law, who was a sympathetic student of Goethe's writings, and of German literature generally. As Scott said of him, Goethe had not a more devout admirer than this young connection of his. It was on the occasion of Lockhart's return from Weimar that he first made the acquaintance of his future father-in-law. It was in the month of May, 1818, when Lockhart called on Scott in Edinburgh. The subject of conversation was naturally Germany and its literature, and Goethe in particular. Lockhart told him that when he arrived in Weimar he enquired of the waiter at the hotel if he knew whether Goethe was then in town. The man stared at Lockhart as if he had never heard the name before. When Lockhart added, "Goethe, the great poet," the waiter shook his head as much in doubt as before. Just then the hostess came to the rescue, saying, " Perhaps the gentleman means ' Herr Geheimrat von Goethe'!" Scott was highly amused and said : " I hope you will come to visit me at Abbotsford one of these days, but when you reach Selkirk or Melrose, be sure you ask even the landlady for nobody but ' the Sheriff'."

Lockhart further informs us that Scott was especially interested when he told him that his first sight of Goethe was as he stepped out of his carriage, laden with wild flowers and plants which he had gathered on the Jena hills on his morning ride. " I am glad," said Scott, " that my old master has pursuits somewhat akin to my own. I am no botanist, properly speaking, and though a dweller on the banks of the Tweed, shall never be knowing about Flora's beauties ; but how I should like to have a talk with him about trees!"

Lockhart seems to have been much impressed by his interview with Goethe, whose very appearance called forth admiration, and remarked to Scott "how much any one must be struck with the majestic beauty of Goethe's countenance; —(the noblest certainly by far that I have yet seen.)"

Long after this visit—to be exact, in 1827—when Eckermann asked Goethe if he still remembered Lockhart, Goethe replied : "Oh, yes, very well ! His personality makes such a distinct impression that one cannot forget it so soon. He must be, as I gather from English travellers, and from my daughter-in-law, a young man of whom good things in literature are to be expected."

184

Lockhart was one of the select band of Goethe disciples to whom Carlyle presented one of the four medals sent for Goethe's well-wishers. " His love of German literature," testified Carlyle, " and debts to you in particular, he has omitted no opportunity of acknowledging." The other recipients of the medals seem to have been Professor Moir, Lord Jeffrey, and Professor Wilson. The last named hardly deserved one from his treatment of Goethe in " Noctes Ambrosianae."

Scott never lost his interest in, or admiration for his " Master " as he always called Goethe. " Faust " continued to exert a certain fascination for him. Lockhart, for example, relates how one morning when he was staying at Abbotsford along with a considerable company of friends, the house was astir betimes, for Scott was an early riser. " Presently," says Lockhart, " Scott hailed me at the casement, and said he had observed a volume of a new edition of Goethe on my table—would I lend it him for a little? He carried off the volume accordingly, and retreated with it to his den. It contained the 'Faust,' and, I believe, in a more complete shape than he had before seen that masterpiece of his old favourite. When we met at breakfast a couple of hours after, he was full of the poem—dwelt with enthusiasm on the airy beauty of its lyrics, the terrible pathos of the scene before the Mater Dolorosa, and the deep skill shown in the various subtle shadings of character between Mephistophiles and poor Margaret. He remarked, however, of the Introduction (which I suspect was new to him) that blood would out—that, consummate artist as he was, Goethe was a German, and that nobody but a German would ever have provoked a comparison with the book of

186

Job, ' the grandest poem that ever was written.' He added that he suspected the end of the story had been left "in obscuro," from despair to match the closing scene of our own Marlowe's Doctor Faustus. Mr Wilson mentioned a report that Coleridge was engaged on a translation of the ' Faust,' ' I hope it is so,' said Scott ; ' Coleridge made Schiller's Wallenstein far finer than he found it, and so he will do by this'." The reader does not require to be informed that this design, like so many of Coleridge's grand projects, was never realised.

While Goethe was enjoying a pleasant old age, surrounded by every material comfort that he desired, with troops of friends and admirers to soothe and flatter him, engaged in the contemplation of a life that somehow afforded him little cause for remorse, his great Scottish admirer, Sir Walter Scott, was bringing to a close a life altogether different, and in quite another manner. It looked like a defeated life, but let us wait the issue! The call came first to Goethe, and the news, when it reached Scott, moved him greatly. He was then cruising in the Mediterranean in the vain search for health. He had been anxious to return home, before the intelligence reached Naples, and it renewed his impatience to do so. "Alas! for Goethe!" were his words, "but he at least died at home. Let us to Abbotsford!"

One touching fact may be recorded here. On this journey home, when passing through Germany, Scott wrote what his son, Charles, endorses as "the last letter written by my father." It is a courteous note to Arthur Schopenhauer, the famous philosopher, then living at Frankfurt-on-Main, regretting that he was too unwell to receive Schopenhauer's visit. There could be little in common between the great-hearted Scotsman and the sour pessimist, but it is an interesting fact that he whose work as a writer began by admiration of German literature should pen his last words to a German philosopher. The late Andrew Lang wrote : " The note is clearly written and well expressed. It is in the Laing MSS. in Edinburgh University." (" Sir Walter Scott," p. 242.)

The following letter appeared in the *Kelso Mail* of June 18, 1832. It is from a correspondent (whose name is not given), from Rome, under date of May 17, 1832. It appears under the heading of " Miscellaneous."

" SIR WALTER SCOTT. Last week Sir Walter Scott left this city, intending to return to Abbotsford by way of Florence, Venice, Munich, Stuttgard, Frankfort, Cologne, Holland, and England. On the whole his residence in Italy has been very beneficial to him, though the effects of the severe paralytic stroke will probably never be wholly removed, as the lameness in his foot was much increased, and he speaks with difficulty. Those who are able perfectly to follow him as he speaks, soon perceive that the intellectual stream still flows in uninterrupted purity, rapidity, and strength. This is also proved by his activity ; besides one work he has already sent home — ' The Siege of Malta ' — he is now putting the last hand to a Calabrian novel — ' Bizarro ' — which is founded on the extraordinary adventures of a very formidable bandit chief. He greatly regrets the death of Goethe, because, as he expressed himself, ' *he would have been so happy to see by his own fireside the powerful genius on whom the world turned.*' Sir Walter received an invitation to Weimar the very week that Goethe died. If he attended only to his health, he would

From Seb. Brant's Book, "The Ship of Fools,"
the first German book translated into English
by Alexander Barclay, a native of Scotland.

return by sea ; but he is drawn by an irresistible longing to the romantic mountains and antique castles that look down into the blue waves of Father Rhine."

The italics above are in the original, and are significant.

The two great writers, Goethe and Sir Walter Scott, died in the same year — 1832 — Goethe in March, when the husbandmen were casting the seed into the ground ; Scott in September, when the reapers were in the fields gathering the harvest. There is a parable in these facts which he who has studied the lives of both men will easily read. Time and death have linked the two men together, and the year 1832, which by the death of Scott marks an era in English literature (as Stopford Brooke reminds us), brings to a close, by Goethe's death, the most glorious period in the literature of Germany.

Conclusion.

IN the foregoing chapters we have shown what a strong influence German writers and especially Goethe, exercised upon the development of Sir Walter Scott's genius. Through his whole literary career, from the time that he made his first attempts at authorship down to the close of his life, that influence was great. A few general remarks may be made in conclusion regarding the nature of the influence.

In the first place it was of a purely literary character. Scott's early ambition to become an author received an impulse from German sources. He saw in the new Germany that seemed to be dawning, vast possibilities of which he was not slow to take advantage. His intense admiration for Goethe was maintained throughout his life, but it should be remembered that that admiration was for Goethe as the literary artist. Carlyle was also much influenced by Goethe but the influence was of quite a different kind; it was personal, and affected Carlyle's mode of thinking and his spiritual attitude, changing, as he admits, his whole outlook in life. Goethe had no such effect upon Scott. Sir Walter praised Goethe, and frankly admitted his obligations to him, but it was always as the author, not as the teacher. He received no spiritual impulse from the sage of Weimar, and his knowledge of Goethe the author was practically confined to his early works. Goethe's greatest works like "Faust" and "Wilhelm Meister," which Carlyle translated into English, made no deep appeal to Sir Walter Scott, and he made no use of these works in his own writings. The truth is, Scott was a romancist from his earliest years and remained so to the end.

It may make the matter clearer if it is pointed out that Goethe's life is divisible into three periods. In the first period he was a romancist and wrote "Werters Leiden" (Sorrows of Werter), the romantic ballads, "Goetz von Berlichingen," etc. The second period dates from his sojourn in Italy which had such an effect on him that he called his visit to Italy a "new birth." He then becomes a classicist. His literary and artistic ideals were completely altered as we see in "Tasso," "Iphigenie auf Tauris," and other works of this period. The third period may be called philosophical; it was in this period that he wrote "West-Eastern Divan," and the second part of "Faust," and other writings of a more or less didactic character.

194

Now, it was to Goethe of the first, or romantic period, that Scott was drawn. Goethe's other writings had little attraction for him, and he made no use of them. Carlyle might write acknowledging his indebtedness to Goethe in such language as this : —

" If I have been delivered from darkness into any measure of light, if I know aught of myself, and my duties and destination, it is to the study of your writings, more than to any other circumstance, that I owe this ; it is you more than any other man that I should always thank and reverence with the feeling of a disciple to his master, nay, of a son to his spiritual Father."

Such language would have been utterly unintelligible to Scott. He did not need the help of Goethe to resolve his religious doubts, if he ever had any. One lesson which Carlyle believed he received from

Goethe—that doubt is best resolved by action—had been practised by Scott all his life. "Scott the very incarnation of Romanticism," says Sir J. R. Seely, "Scott of all great modern poets the most completely a stranger to the whole Hellenic world—read and imitated Goethe when as yet no other Englishman did. He translated 'Goetz von Berlichingen' in 1799, and the influence of that play is traceable in 'Ivanhoe,' as 'Mignon' is imitated in 'Peveril of the Peak,' and perhaps also in the harper of 'Wilhelm Meister' in the 'Lay of the Last Minstrel' He spoke of Goethe as his master, and does this not naturally lead us to think of Goethe as a great light of the romantic school? Scott's biographer thinks that but for 'Goetz,' the idea might never have flashed upon Scott's mind that his own legendary lore might be worked up into poems and romances."

A great wave of romanticism was passing over Europe at the time that Scott began to write. In the case of many writers this romantic spirit evaporated in mere sentiment and their works after a time passed into oblivion. The romantic element appealed to Scott, but he was not carried away by it and could use it for his own purposes. He turned first to Goethe who helped him most, but we have seen that other German writers were industriously explored. We have mentioned some of these who all belonged to the romantic school, Bürger, Schiller, Herder, Wieland, Fouque, Kotzebue, Hoffmann, etc. Scott knew the romantic literature of the eighteenth and early nineteenth centuries better perhaps than any man of his day, and any one who helped him to extend this knowledge was most gratefully received by him. He loved German literature, he said, but he was a discriminating reader and was alive to its weakness and its extravagances.

He understood also the characteristics of the German people and could describe them with wonderful accuracy although he never lived in Germany. The country and its people had always a great attraction for him, but he was no blind admirer of men and things German. He makes that openly evident in his borrowings and the use he made of them.

While the effect of Scott's German studies and German sympathies is seen in his writings, we look in vain for any trace of it in the man himself. He selected and marshalled materials gathered from various writers, chiefly contemporaries, with much skill, but he never allowed himself to be biased by them ; his political views underwent no change ; his patriotism suffered no abatement ; his style never became Germanised, as did that of Carlyle.

It is as a literary artist then, that we have to consider him when speaking of German influence. Hence the title of these articles which seek to trace that influence on his literary productions, not on the man himself. Scott was wholly unaffected by German philosophy, German religion, German politics. It could not be said of him what Goethe once said of Carlyle. "He is almost as much German as ourselves."

There have been great changes in the world since Scott began his literary career by translating a German ballad. Nations have risen and fallen ; Empires have been lifted off their hinges, but these two writers, Scott and Goethe, retain their high position. Time, the great destroyer, is powerless against their fame. Where shall we look for their successors to-day?

Appendix I.

"DOUSTERSWIVEL."

(See "Germans and Germany," p. 38, and "The Antiquary," p. 63).

Who was "Dousterswivel"? Had this notorious character, of whom Scott makes such ample use in the Antiquary, a prototype, or was he purely a creature of the imagination? Scott was not given to create imaginary beings. His method was to take some real person and magnify or embellish the characteristics or peculiarities of that person, or the chief incidents of his life, in such a way as to excite the interest of his readers. Dousterswivel is so minutely described that we cannot doubt he was a real person.

Reference was made in a former chapter to Rudolf Eric Raspe in connection with

"Baron Munchausen," and the evidence is convincing that Raspe was the man whom Scott had in his mind when he described Dousterswivel and his doings. Raspe was born in Hanover in 1737, educated at Göttingen and Leipzig, where he acquired considerable fame as an archaeologist. He gained an appointment in the University and Library at Hanover, probably through his great knowledge of English. When he afterwards became secretary to the University of Göttingen he published translations from Latin and French philosophers, as well as the poems of Ossian and Percy's "Reliques." Later, in 1767, he became professor of archaeology and chief librarian in Cassel. His works on natural history, mineralogy, and archaeology were widely received and he was elected an honorary member of the Royal Society of London. He was then at the height of his fame, but from this point his fortunes declined. Entrusted with a commission to Italy to purchase gems and coins for the Cassel Collection, he proved unfaithful to his trust and disappeared. In the warrant that was issued for his apprehension he is thus described : "Councillor Raspe, a long-faced man, with small eyes, crooked nose, red hair under his stumpy periwig, and a jerky gait." This may be compared with Scott's description of Dousterswivel: "A tall, beetle-browed, awkward-built man, who entered upon scientific subjects with more assurance than knowledge." He was captured in the Hartz mountains, but escaped and made his way to London. He gained the friendship and pecuniary assistance of Horace Walpole and published several scientific and literary works. But his character was undermined by his actions, and his name was struck from the roll of membership of the Royal

Society. Still, he succeeded in getting an appointment as Assay-master at tin mines in Cornwall, where he wrote the first version of "Baron Munchausen." He published also a work on ancient and modern gems in 1790 at Edinburgh. When in Scotland he persuaded Sir John Sinclair, of the "Statistical Account," that his estate at Ulbster, in Caithness, contained valuable minerals, as Dousterswivel persuaded Sir Arthur Wardour in Scott's narrative. Other Scottish proprietors were deceived in like manner and rumours spread widely regarding the untold mineral wealth of this country, as may be seen from the "Scots Magazine" of 1789 and 1791. Thus, to quote only a few lines: "Mr Raspe, the German mineralogist, after having examined the greater part of the Western Highlands and Islands, has at last begun his survey in Caithness. He has been very successful in discovering mines in copper, lead, iron, cobalt, manganese, etc., and he will probably publish an account of these discoveries. . . . On the whole, it is believed that the tour of this ingenious traveller will turn out of great public as well as private utility and will do credit to those who have promoted it."

Then Raspe decamped ! He next turns up in Ireland, where he died in 1794. His life was a romance of extraordinary cleverness and roguery, of which we have here given but the barest outlines. In the "Advertisement " to the Antiquary, Scott says : " The knavery of the Adept in the following sheets may appear forced and improbable ; but we have had very late instances of the force of superstitious credulity to a much greater extent, and the reader may be assured that this part of the narrative is founded on a fact of actual occurrence." Scott probably got

much of his information through Sir John
Sinclair, with whom he had some correspondence, as well as from the "Scots
Magazine," and from Scotch lairds whom
the scoundrelly German had victimised.

Raspe died in the same year as his
friend Bürger, who is believed to have
helped him with "Munchausen," and
who as the author of "Lenore" forms
a further link with Scott.

Appendix II.

THE LAMENT OF THE NOBLE LADY OF ASAN AGA.

(See "Translations of German Ballads," p. 5).

This translation by Sir Walter Scott of Goethe's "Klagegesang von der edlen Frauen des Asan Aga," is not included in English editions of Scott's works, and is therefore not generally known here.

What yonder glimmers so white on the mountain,
    Glimmers so white where yon sycamores grow?
Is it wild swans around Vaga's fair fountain?
    Or is it a wreath of the wintery snow?

Had it been snow glimmers white on the mountain
    By this it had melted before the bright day,
Or had it been swans around Vaga's fair fountain,
    They had stretch'd their broad pinions and sped them
        away.

It is not then swans round the fountain of Vaga,
    It is not a wreath of the wintery snow,
But it is the gay tents of the fierce Asan Aga,
    Glimmering so white where yon sycamores grow.

Low lies the Chief on the couch of the wounded,
    There watch his sisters with tenderest care,
There weeps his mother in sorrow unbounded,
    Every sad friend—but his Lady—is there.

She sorrow'd more than the fondest of mothers,
    But from the thronged camp in which wounded he lay,
Though there flocked sad friends, tender sisters and
        brothers,
    Timid shamefacedness compell'd her to stay.

But at her absence high kindling his anger
    Wrote the stern Chieftain this severing line—
" Away from my castle, its Mistress no longer,
    Away from my children and all that is mine."

Anguish the heart of that lady deep rended,
    When the hard message was brought to her eye ;
Woe were the looks on her children she bended,
    Weeping around her, though scarce knowing why.

O'er the high drawbridge come horses loud prancing,
    Wildly she started in desperate mood,
She thought 'twas the signal of Asan advancing,
    And rush'd to the turret to plunge in the flood.

" Stay thee, oh, stay thee ! My Mother ! My Mother !
    'Tis not the steeds of our father you hear—
'Tis the fleet horse of Carazan, thy brother,"
    Thus cried her children in sorrow and fear,

Then the sad mourner turn'd back to her brother,
  Clinging around him with bitterest moan :
" Late of those five little darlings the mother,
  Now see me, Carazan, the mother of none."

Silent and sad stood her brother, Carazan,
  Then drew from his bosom the severing Bill
Speaking divorce to the Lady of Asan,
  Leaving her free to espouse whom she will.

Then the sad dame to her girls gave her blessing,
  Kissed the red cheek of each fair-featured boy,
But from the suckling to her breast closely pressing—
  Woes me !—she could not unloosen the tie.

Torn was the tie by her harsh-tempered brother ;
  He raised her behind him upon his fleet horse,
And to the lofty abode of their mother
  He bent with the sorrowful lady his course.

Scarce had a fortnight that widow past over,
  Only a fortnight, a fortnight and day—
When to that lady came many a lover,
  All in her mourning as weeping she lay.

The greatest of all was Imoski's proud Cady ;
  Long had he loved her more dearly than life ;
Then to her brother spoke, weeping, that lady—
  " Give me no more to another to wife."

" Give me no more as wife to another "—
  Thus to her brother in sorrow she spoke—
" Lest when my poor orphans shall call on their mother.
  By anguish and longing my heart should be broke."

Her brother cared not for the prayer of the lady,
  Firmly resolv'd to bestow her as spouse—
To bestow her as spouse on Imoski's great Cady,
  That the high marriage gifts might enrich his proud
      house.

" Yet bid the Cady, my brother Carazan,
  Bring a black veil this sad head to enfold,
Lest, when I pass by the dwelling of Asan,
  These widowed eyes should their orphans behold."

Scarce was the message received by the Cady,
  Soon he assembled the gay bridal train,
And bringing the veil as desired by the lady,
  Safely the towers of Carazan they gain.

Safely they gained the high towers of Carazan,
  But with the Bride has returned the gay train—
Lo ! as they pass'd the proud dwelling of Asan,
  The children beheld their lost mother again.

Loudly they shouted, " O art thou returned?
  Com'st thou our meals and our pastimes to share?
O, for thy absence, how long have we mourned !
  Pass on no further—thy children are here."

At the fond voices a sudden pause made she—
  " Rein in your steeds these loved turrets below "—
Thus to the gallants in agony said she—
  " Till my last gifts on my babes I bestow."

Beneath the proud turrets the bridal train rested
  While her last gifts on her babes she bestow'd,
While she the boys with rich girdles invested,
  And with gay sabres with jewels that glowed.

Deck'd she her daughters in silks richly rustling ;
  And for those days when his strength might them wield,
To the dear suckling in her bosom close nestling
  Gave she a girdle, a sabre, and shield.

All this from beside saw the stern Asan Aga,
  And loud to his children he haughtily cried—
" Away from that woman more false than the Vaga,
  More light than its breeze, and more cold than its tide."

Away fled the children for fear loudly crying,
  All but the suckling she clasp'd to her breast—
Down sank the lady, pale, shivering, and dying,
  Grasp'd it yet closer—and sank into rest.

If we compare this translation, or rather paraphrase, with the original we see what great liberties Scott took with his text. His six and twenty quatrains are as unlike Goethe's unrhymed poem, broken into stanzas of from four to eleven lines, as well could be. Goethe's style, too, is highly condensed, the language simple and direct, with none of the rhetorical flourishes in which Scott delights ; the impression on the reader is consequently much greater. In some places Scott either unwittingly, or to "improve" the style, gives the wrong meaning. Not to occupy unnecessary space, I quote only these two lines from Goethe's text, with Scott's rendering.

Und dem Säugling, hülflos, in der Wiege,
Gab sie für die Zukunft auch ein Röckehen.

Nothing could be simpler or clearer than this, but here is Scott's version : —

To the dear suckling in her bosom close nestling,
Gave she a girdle, a sabre, and shield !

Professor Heinemann, of Leipzig, has traced the history of this ballad through many countries and languages. Düntzer thinks that Goethe became acquainted with the legend in 1775 when on a tour in Switzerland. (See my letter in *Scotsman* of Feb. 23, 1924.)

Appendix III.

BARON BUNSEN AND SIR WALTER SCOTT.

A little known passage in the "Memoirs of Baron Bunsen," gives a life-like description of Sir Walter Scott during the last days of his visit to Rome. The passage is given under date of 10th May, 1832, that is, about five months before his death.

" We saw Sir Walter Scott often during the first week of his being here. The first time of meeting a shock was caused, as I was not prepared for his difficulty in speaking ; but, though his animation is gone his conversation is much of the same sort as formerly, therefore most interesting and original, and his expression of goodness and benevolence truly venerable, in the midst of physical decay. He one day dined with us, with his daughter, Sir William Gell and Miss Mackenzie being the rest of the party. Bunsen had taken into consideration what subject would be interesting to Sir Walter Scott, and knowing that popular poetry had always attracted him, he sought out the German ballads, so enthusiastically sung during the 'War of

, Liberation ' in 1813, and after giving him
an idea of the sense, made Henry and
Ernest sing them. Sir Walter was evidently pleased, and observed of that noble
struggle, quoting a verse of the ' Requiem,'
' Tantus labor non sit cassus ! " He called
the two boys to him, and laid a hand upon
the head of each, with a solemn utterance
of ' God bless you ! ' He gave us a kindly
worded invitation to visit him when we
should come to England, saying, ' I have
had losses ; much is changed ; but I have
still ' my two gowns, and all things hand-
some about me,' as Dogberry says."

At taking leave he said, ' I hope your
own feelings will be your reward, for all
the kindness and hospitality you have
shown me.' Once after this we found
him at home, making a morning visit. I
brought him a set of ordinary engravings,
called devotional, relating, of course, to
Madonna worship, such as are universally
spread about Rome, and he made the
observation. ' It ought to be a pure and
mild religion, which finds its objects in a
young woman and a child, the loveliest of
human beings.' I was not a little struck
by this tolerance, and of course made no
reply, but on reflection I make out that he

213

meant to indicate a truth, though a one-sided truth. . . . .

Sir Walter is to depart in two days, if not quite ill by the excursion intended for to-day, when Sir W. Gell will take him to Bracciano, driving from ten o'clock in the burning sun twenty-five miles. He ought not to have remained so late in the South ; but although those around him are nervously anxious about his state, no health regulation would seem to be enforced.

One anecdote more of him : on the occasion of a morning visit, when Bunsen found him alone, with his emaciated-looking son, Charles, silent and unoccupied, in a corner, Sir Walter asked some questions about Goethe, and about his son, who died at Rome in 1830. Bunsen avoided giving the particulars of the manner of his death, caused by habits of intoxication, merely saying that the 'son of Goethe had nothing of his father but the name; ' and was startled by Sir Walter slowly turning his head towards his son, with the words, 'Why, Charles, that is what people will be saying of you !' Alas ! this wreck of a young man is the same being that I remember such an engaging child at Edinburgh in 1810 ! " (Vol. I. p 231.)

G-1